Pitchfork Pulpit

Pitchfork Pulpit

Wisdom and Practice in a Self-Reliant Life

By Joel Salatin

Polyface, Inc.
Swoope, Virginia

This publication is designed to provide accurate and authoritative information in regard to the subject matter covered. It is sold with the understanding that the publisher is not engaged in rendering legal, accounting or other professional service. If legal advice or other expert assistance is required, the services of a competent professional person should be sought.

From a declaration of principles jointly adopted by a committee of the American Bar Association and a committee of publishers.

Pitchfork Pulpit: Wisdom and Practice in a Self-Reliant Life

First Edition, 2025
© 2025 Joel Salatin
All rights reserved.
ISBN: 978-1-7336866-4-8
Library of Congress Control Number: 2025908513

Edited by Jennifer L. Dehoff and Ashley N. McLain.
Cover photos by Rachel Salatin.
Cover design & book layout by Jennifer Dehoff Design.
All rights reserved.

Printed and bound in the USA.

Contents

JOEL SALATIN and his family operate Polyface Farm in Virginia's Shenandoah Valley. His parents purchased the farm in 1961 and developed the basic principles of design and production that now show 60 years' refinement.

Joel gravitated toward communication activities in high school and college, graduating with a BA degree in English, and after a brief journalism hiatus returned to the family farm full time Sept. 24, 1982.

Editor of *The Stockman Grass Farmer* magazine, he writes and speaks around the world on food and farm issues. With a long track record of innovation and excellence, Polyface holds educational seminars, farm tours, day camps and events to encourage duplication and understanding.

This is Joel's 17th book. See a complete list of other books and resources by Joel at the back of this book.

Introduction

By Joel Salatin

I was only 13 years old when John Shuttleworth and friends in North Carolina launched *The Mother Earth News* (*TMEN*) in 1970. I don't remember whether my dad subscribed that first year or not, but I know it was early on and I was extremely young when I began devouring the magazine.

The Plowboy interviews introduced me to A.P. Thomson, the work of Allan Savory and perhaps most significantly, Bill Mollison and Dave Holmgren's Permaculture. Every month the magazine came with do-it-yourself projects and non-chemical solutions to virtually everything. I spent hours combing those pages and dreaming about leveraging all that advice and wisdom someday as a fulltime farmer.

I still have clipped articles in my filing cabinets. "Kon Tipi" about a family that constructed their house for under $2,000 using long poles and a canvas cover guaranteed for 15 years. Their point was that even if it all had to be rebuilt in 15 years, they enjoyed debt-free living all that time to accumulate cash or other equity. Raised bed gardening. John Jeavons and French Intensive gardening. Every compost turner you could imagine.

Our conservative Christian family was not on the hippie spectrum politically or socially, but all of our farm friends hewed to that cloth. *TMEN* and the Bible enjoyed togetherness on my nightstand. Our family opposed the Viet Nam war from day one, although most of our social and church friends agreed with the Pentagon.

Our family had deep friendships with beaded, bearded, braless hippies during those years; we often conversed about information *TMEN* brought to us. The magazine framed much of my stewardship ethic philosophy and brought to our family practical projects from that caretaking paradigm. How to build compost piles. How to stack animals in complementary ecological and economic symbiosis.

By the time I was 18 and Virginia Tech's poultry science department did everything possible to recruit me into their agriculture program, I had zero interest in learning the industrial model; I was steeped in *TMEN* protocols. Chickens on pasture. Cows eating grass. Tomatoes growing in compost. It was all in the magazine, feeding my head, heart, hands, and health (the 4-H motto). In short, I drank *TMEN* Kool-aid. Our own on-farm experiments verified everything we read in those pages.

Like many ventures, when the founders retired and sold the magazine, it went through some wanderings, becoming more urbanized and leaving its roots. Many people left its subscriber base during the 1990s and early 2000s. But in around 2010, under new ownership and leadership, it returned (in my opinion) to its roots and experienced a revival. It was like *TMEN* came home and folks like me responded enthusiastically with subscriptions and participation in their physical fairs. For years, *TMEN* was not only the big dog; it was the only dog in the homestead renaissance movement.

With this background, then, imagine my euphoria when in 2014 the staff asked me to write a column for the magazine. As a farmer/writer/homesteader, this was paradise. I couldn't go any higher. I had arrived.

We decided to call the column Pitchfork Pulpit and the staff gave me unlimited latitude to address whatever issue was on my radar. I did hard core how-to stuff, political stuff, spiritual stuff, social stuff. What an honor and privilege to write for the magazine that had provided such foundational projects and thinking in my own development. Because this was such a huge publication and leader in the homestead field, I chose topics carefully and wandered across the do-it-yourself landscape strategically.

The 50-year anniversary issue in January 2020 sported me on the cover, extolling my long loving relationship with the magazine. What an honor. We began planning a first ever on-farm *TMEN* fair here at Polyface, preparing to host thousands of people over a two-day extravaganza.

Unfortunately, the magazine parted with me during the upheavals of 2020. The covid crisis and other social and political differences came between us and the column was terminated. In all, it was a six-year run and generated some of my best writing—at least, that's what I thought.

In the time since, I've wanted to preserve those columns as part of my writing legacy and this book is the result of that desire. It's not as long as it would have been had my *TMEN* run been longer, but these pithy columns address things every homesteader spends time contemplating. Sometimes the magazine editorial staff suggested topics and sometimes I wrote from my own conversations with people.

I've always written not for my benefit, but for the benefit of others. What are the needs I'm hearing from other people? What are their concerns? How can I help? If someone expresses a need, you can be pretty sure other people share it.

To get all these columns and these years of thinking in one place gives me one more offering for our culture's greater need: to come home, to our farms, our gardens, our kitchens, and our neighborhoods. This collection of columns, I hope, will facilitate that cultural shift, bringing intentional living back to our homes and hearts. Thank you for adding this collection to your library. If you're ever nearby, come by for a visit.

Joel Salatin
Polyface Farm
Swoope, VA

Pitchfork Pulpit

Wisdom and Practice in a Self-Reliant Life

Price Elitism

written in 2014

We live in a world of sound bites. The long discourse that dominated pre-television days seldom happens any more. If someone disagrees with you, their attention span to listen to your argument lasts about one minute. If you can't score a point in that amount of time, the conversation is over.

Being able to dispel wrong-headed thinking in sound bites is now the holy grail in argumentation. We have plenty of wrong-headed thinking to counter. One of the most common misperceptions, and extremely frustrating, is the notion that people like me are food snobs. That in fact I'm some sort of elitist if I patronize local compost-fertilized multi-speciated pasture-based produce and meats.

This notion is perpetuated even among my friends. Perhaps the most egregious example was in the blockbuster documentary *Food Inc.* when the Hispanic family stopped at Burger King for dinner and then lamented their inability to buy fresh produce at the supermarket. Although I haven't been to Burger King in 35 years, I know how much that meal cost.

With that super duper soft drink, fries, and deluxe burger, it was easily $10.

For that amount of money, that family could buy two whole pounds of our farm's grass-finished premier world class ground beef. I guarantee you two pounds of our ground beef has more nutrition than that Burger King meal. This is not to pick on Burger King. I don't begrudge people eating there. What I begrudge is people eating there because they think it's cheap and then telling me they can't afford my product because it's expensive.

The result is a victim mentality that permeates every food discussion. The idea that people can't afford good food is practically axiomatic in our collective thinking. Because often the sticker price of my integrity food is more than the sticker price of industrial supermarket fare, I'm tempted to react apologetically, head down, guilty as charged. I think a lot of us in this integrity food movement are like that—we even allow ourselves deep down to believe the "I can't" mentality.

So I've been thinking. Can we sound bite our way into a discussion about the price of food? Can we articulate a charitable non-offensive answer that challenges this allegation of elitism? I don't know if I have an answer, but I have some proposals I'd like to try on for size. Each sound bite is a question, not a direct assault.

1. Have you bought anything recently you didn't need?
Most people think their purchases are wise and necessary. Ask someone to help you formulate a list of common and unnecessary purchases. Here are some, in no particular order:

   • Starbucks (if you spend $10 per day per work week, that's $2,500 annually).

- Alcohol
- Designer jeans with holes already in the knees
- Tobacco
- People magazine
- Lottery tickets
- Political fundraising dinners
- Movie tickets

We can stop the list there, but you get the idea. I'm convinced people are far quicker to assume they have no choice than to appreciate discretionary spending is real . . . and huge. Show me the home without any of these items and you won't find many. Generally the discussion about integrity food prices gets derailed immediately because we don't have an answer for every single situation. The whole discussion focuses on the tiny fraction of the population in hardship rather than the majority who routinely buy unneeded things and then claim good food is too expensive. This includes many if not most who are officially below the poverty line.

The saying "pick the low-hanging fruit first" applies here. Certainly hardship cases exist. But they are so few, let's deal with the discretionary stuff—the easy picking—first. Letting the discussion quickly veer into the most egregious hardship cases without appreciating how many people can choose to change is like refusing to pick apples from a tree until we've figured out how to pick the most difficult apple in the tippy-top. We need to keep the conversation targeted to the doable first; sometimes the difficult parts take care of themselves by default.

2. Have you cooked a meal from scratch? The notion that processed food is cheap is simply not true. I was at the New

York City Green Market a couple of years ago, arguably the most elite artisanal food mecca in our country. I asked my host to take me to the most expensive potatoes at the market.

She took me to a potato vendor whose display looked like it should be in the Museum of Modern Art (MOMA), another special place in New York City. The roughly one foot square partitioned wooden boxes held some 20 varieties of potatoes. Round, long, gnarly, red, yellow, white, blue. It was truly a masterpiece of bounty and variety.

I looked over the display and found the most expensive potato. It was a blue fingerling for $2 a pound. Follow me here—this was the most expensive potato in the most expensive market in the U.S. How many potatoes in your neighborhood supermarket are selling for twice that price—as potato chips?

Processed food is expensive. If you price microwavable frozen boxes of chicken nuggets in the shape of Dino the Dinosaur, you'll find that it's more expensive than pastured local whole chicken.

Ah, but you have to prepare that blue fingerling potato in your kitchen to make potato chips at half the price of store-bought. And I hear the whining: "But I don't want to cook a whole chicken." That's personal discretion. The key to affordable food is to reclaim domestic culinary arts. Getting in your kitchen to prepare, process, package, and preserve food is not a sentence to the dark ages of hoop skirts, wash boards, and open hearth cooking—as romantic as that may sound to somebody who never did it.

Today's kitchens are not like grandma's. We have hot and cold running water; we don't have to run to the creek for water. We have stainless steel, refrigeration, electric skillets, ovens that turn on faster than wood stoves. We have Cuisinarts, timed bake, bread makers, crockpots, and ice cream makers. Goodness, our modern kitchens are techno-gadgetized up the wazoo. And all these conveniences beg to be used—hear them chirping from the cupboards?

3. What is more valuable to you than integrity food for your children? This is the time part of price. Time and money have always gone hand-in-hand. My challenge to get in the kitchen usually results in a temper tantrum about not enough time. Too often it's from a soccer mom who has no problem carting the 6-year-olds 3 hours one way to a tournament and then 3 hours home and stopping for Happy Meals because she doesn't have time to cook.

Again, let's be willing to call choice what it is. We all make choices. The notion that we can build integrity into our food system without a cultural shift in behavior is fundamentally flawed. The choices are subtle. Waiting to take the Caribbean cruise until after the tomatoes have frosted allows you to get that pre-frost bounty in the larder so it doesn't go to waste.

Modern sophisticated Americans have abdicated visceral participation with food. The inevitable and obvious result is food that your great-grandma would not recognize. Another result is ignorance about food. Ignorance breeds fear. Many Americans fear food these days, afraid to thaw chicken or afraid of butternut squash with some dirt particles on the outside. When you work with food, knowledge replaces ignorance and faith replaces fear.

4. Have you grown anything yourself? Certainly some folks would have a hard time growing something, but that's a pretty small number. Any pet could be replaced with two chickens to eat kitchen scraps and lay eggs in return. That's the cheapest and best food you can imagine.

Container gardening is cool. Stackable containers are even cooler. Raised beds in the backyard, with season extension floating row covers under plastic tunnels allow unprecedented season extension and on-site food integrity. How about selling the flat screen TV and using that money to install a simple solarium on the south side of the house? Passive solar and hardy greens all winter. Not a bad trade.

Compost and perlite on the roof to grow veggies there. Warmer in winter due to the R-factor and cooler in summer with transpiring leaves. Honey bees on the porch roof. Gardens in every vacant urban lot. Edible landscaping—it doesn't take any more work to grow an apple tree than a flowering ornamental. Replace the roses with tomatoes. A do-it-yourself dinner is the cheapest one you'll ever have, and if the cost is less couch potato time, you've replaced a life liability with a health-giving asset. How much better could it get?

Sound bite questions by nature can help all of us grapple with opposing views. These are some that I've found helpful in the elitism food snob debate. I hope you can adapt them to your conversations to re-build integrity in our food system. Let's empower some victims.

2

Not Old Fashioned

written in 2014

C alling something old fashioned encourages tourists and antique buyers, but it does not describe a world people want to live in with 9 billion people. When it comes to food and farming, old fashioned does not captivate the hearts and minds of our culture.

I think too often the earth-stewardship movement, if I may use that term broadly, positions itself as returning to a bygone era, to the good old days, to pre-electricity and pre-petroleum. While wash boards, hoop skirts, and hearth cooking may have a romantic appeal to some, living this way does not capture and inspire the imagination of today's solution seekers.

Even people who yearn for simpler times and a simpler lifestyle don't want to go there without electricity and automobiles. Those of us who yearn for a different world to live in need a catalyst message dynamic enough to convert fast food junkies. The industrial food system spends a lot of time refining its message. Along with denigrating do-it-yourselfing, pastured livestock, and compost piles, it embraces words like technology, futuristic, and feeding the world.

These all have emotional appeal. Savvy people like to

hitch themselves to that kind of engine. Solving problems, meeting needs, going places—these phrases capture hearts and minds. If one thing can kill a movement, it's to be thought of as stodgy, anti-tech, and stuck in old ways.

This is a ticklish messaging point for those of us dedicated to proven earth stewardship principles that predate electricity and petroleum. Part of our worldview is that in a horse race, you bet on the proven winner. Carbon-centric soil building rather than chemical-centric, for example, is a proven winner. But how do you identify your methodology that mimics nature without sounding backward and unscientific?

As I see more and more anti-ecology emanating from the industry and government agencies, I lie awake at night trying to figure out sound bite positive messaging. If I decry Smithfield's sale to the Chinese, I'm either xenophobic or childishly protectionist. If I decry genetically modified organisms, I'm anti-science. If I disagree with food safety policy that criminalizes an artisan who sells home-made yoghurt to a friend at church, I'm an anarchist.

The roots for this perception that our movement is backward is deep. The early 1970s back-to-the-land movement that spawned *The Mother Earth News* and many others started with the word back. The struggles that these souls experienced, from lost money to lost fantasies, testify to the stark reality that going back is not something most of us want to do.

So what kind of messaging; what kind of lexicon works? It has to be big enough, sacred enough, and innovative enough to capture the heart of thinking people. How do you in effect stop a person in his tracks—a person content to watch TV sports all weekend, depend on pharmaceuticals for every malady, and assume all is well in the world as long as the Kardashians' dysfunction continues to provide interesting conversation material?

I think our side needs to position itself as new-fashioned. We have said no to GMOs, chemical fertilizers, Concentrated Animal Feeding Operations (CAFOs), and unpronounceable food additives. I know it's hard to believe, but these things have become the old fashion, and we need to call them that. They are outdated and falling apart, just like a neglected building. Anyone who thinks we can continue inventing new generations of drugs faster than micro-organisms can adapt is simply guilty of Neanderthal thinking.

Here are some words I think we can use to create contrast, but do it in a way that stimulates conversations and more than passing interest in our solutions.

1. Integrated food and farming rather than segregated. Both of these are powerful social words. Who wants to be in favor of segregation? And yet that is exactly what city ordinances forbidding backyard chickens are about. Yes, long ago chickens ate food scraps because a garbage truck didn't come and take potato skins to the landfill. How could we ever have invented such a segregated system?

Integration is hip; it's what people intuitively know is the right thing to do. When I encounter someone who opposes urban chickens, I love to look her in the eye and ask: "Why are you such a segregationist?" Now that, dear people, gets a reaction. And that's what we need to try to do. Powerful positive words move people. Integrated food systems are fundamentally superior to segregated ones.

2. Caressing food systems rather than Conquistador.
Universally, Conquistadors and Crusaders have negative
emotional equity. Who wants to be one of those people?
Juxtapose that with a caress. Our side touches ecology with a
caress that teases out of our nest abundance based on respect
and voluntary consent. We do not take by wrestling with our
ecological womb as if it is a reluctant partner, to be subdued
violently and forcefully.

Yes, we do run chainsaws and broadforks and chipper-
shredders, but the goal of our disturbance is thoughtful
stewardship. Thoughtfulness guides our every movement. I
never cease to be amazed at the number of farmers I see
locating hay feeders and mineral troughs in a valley rather than
on a hillside. These congregation points accumulate manure--
why wouldn't you want that blessing up on a hillside instead of
down in a valley where the first rain will wash it away?

3. Healing rather than hurting. Here at Polyface, our cooler
bags are imprinted with the phrase "healing the planet one bite
at a time." Almost everyone wants to heal rather than hurt.
Compost heals soil and feeds earthworms; chemical fertilizer
scalds earthworms, burning them alive. Pastured livestock
virtually dances in the field. When you enter a factory animal
facility, you don't see dancing beings. They cannibalize each
other in their boredom. It's sad.

Here's the point, though. We don't pasture livestock
because it is old-fashioned. We do it because it makes happy,
healthy animals. It's the new-fashioned way to farm. Out
with the old, in with the new. It provides all sorts of benefits,
including biomass recycling, exercise, fulfillment, and superior

nutrition, both for the animal and the human who ultimately partakes.

On our farm, we do not let people even whisper to each other: "This is like grandpa's farm." If I hear it, I'll interrupt and diplomatically start a lesson about being new-fashioned. I've even put together a program for civic clubs highlighting why ours is not grandpa's farm.

I take a box of props. Here are some of the objects:

1. Electric fence energizer. Grandpa couldn't move his cows every day to customize biomass pruning and stimulate sunbeam conversion to sequestered carbon. Now with computer micro-chipped energizers, we can.

2. Polyethylene pipe. Grandpa couldn't deliver clean, potable water to the far reaches of his farm. With this material, we can keep animals out of riparian areas, irrigate, and send water over the undulations of the land. Amazing.

3. Shade cloth. Grandpa couldn't provide portable shelter because roofing was too heavy and susceptible to wind damage. This new-fangled material lets the wind blow through and the fabric weighs practically nothing.

4. Solar-friendly polymers for solariums and green houses. Grandpa relied on the larder for winter food. These new materials enable season extension and passive solar gain at low cost and high efficiency.

Rather than promoting a return to old fashioned, celebrating the solutions in our new-fashioned techno-glitzy eco-caress world gives us the message of hope and progress.

We don't want to stop the clock; we want to be on time for tomorrow's needs. Nobody does it better than composters, do-it-yourselfers, and foodscape savvy practitioners. Now let's go to the future.

3

Hoarding or Hydrating

written in 2015

Rain barrels, cisterns, ponds, springs, streams, aquifers: manmade and natural water interfaces create interesting conversations.

Although everyone agrees that water is a foundational and precious resource, we diverge greatly on how humans should interact with it. On my many trips to Australia, arguably the driest continent on the earth, I'm always struck by the cisterns adjacent to every roof. Even in highly urban areas, large cisterns holding 3,000-15,000 gallons of water snuggle up underneath roof guttering downspouts.

Contrast that with Colorado's prohibition against rain barrels and the divergent views toward water become apparent. California is considering meters on all wells in order to regulate aquifer depletion. Some groups want to destroy dams in rivers to restore the natural water course.

In a recent discussion with a landowner, I proposed building a couple of ponds in a valley. Although the valley bottom stays dry nearly all summer, from late fall until late spring it sports a tiny run-off stream. I suggested these ponds could be used for irrigation in the summer or simply to add transpiration and seepage capacity to enhance the atmospheric and geologic water cycle.

With a puzzled look, she asked: "But won't the ponds deny water to people downstream? Will streams and springs down stream still have enough water?" This question went to the crux of the tension between hoarding and hydrating. Beyond that, it illustrates the tension between private ownership and the commons.

Anyone versed in environmental stewardship understands the concept of the commons. Much has been written about the "tragedy of the commons" wherein what is commonly owned tends to be abused. If we want good land stewardship, we need private ownership to incentivize investment--so says the American capitalist.

On the other hand, a stream that traverses my property is part of the commons. If everyone who owns property abutting that stream sticks a pipe in and begins sucking water, eventually the stream won't exist. People downstream yell "Foul" and demand relief. Rightly so.

How do we resolve this tension between water I can rightly call mine versus the water that's part of the commons? How we interact with water says a lot about how we interact with all of nature, our neighbors, and our view of earth stewardship.

Does a pond actually reduce water downstream or enhance it? Does it deplete the commons or increase the commons? Let's agree that if a policy increases the commons, it's probably a good thing because that means there's more for everyone. If we could figure out a way to increase fresh air, increase pure water, increase soil—those would all be good things.

P. A. Yeomans, the Australian who developed the keyline system and wrote the iconic *Water for Every Farm* more than half a century ago believed that the weak link on every landscape was hydration. Australia, like the U.S., was settled by people from temperate Europe—primarily the British Isles— where agricultural productivity often required dehydration. Drainage was more important than hydration.

But in Australia and America, the overwhelming need is hydration, not drainage. This British Isles perception, however, is still apparent in our culture. A pond is all but illegal in much of the U.S., especially in more arid areas. As if simple perceptions about water weren't enough of a problem, today people often view ponds as attractive nuisances (what if a child drowns in one?) or harbingers of avian influenza (beware those ducks—they might carry disease).

Any study of keyline water design or permaculture, however, debunks these perceptions as fundamentally flawed. Landscape hydration requires that we keep raindrops as close to where they fall for as long as possible. The faster raindrops head downhill in their gravitational journey to the ocean, the less they can be used to moisten the earth to keep earthworms functioning to keep plants growing to harvest more sunlight and sequester more carbon.

Raindrops that don't hang around create erosion, flooding, and deserts. Holding raindrops that would otherwise cascade downhill actually adds to the net water holding capacity of the ecosystem. Ponds add evaporative moisture to the atmosphere, increasing humidity and cloud-forming capacity. Ponds help maintain spring and stream flow in dry times, not only by seeping slightly into the landscape but also by providing useful water for irrigation.

To the landowner fearful that a pond would deprive water downstream, I explained that a pond catches only surface runoff. Yeomans contended that every farm should strive to eliminate surface runoff. The reason that doesn't deplete the system is because surface runoff only occurs when retentive capacity is full. In other words, when it rains, the soil sponges up the raindrops. When the sponge is saturated or for whatever reason (too hard, for example) can't absorb any more raindrops, that excess water becomes a liability. It carves gullies, carries off nutrients and soil, and in extreme cases can cause flooding problems downstream.

Think of the water holding capacity in a given area as a cup. It starts pouring rain. The cup fills and runs over. The cup represents the commons. The excess represents damage to the commons. Once the commons is full, the excess, I would submit, is my water—private property. Investing in another cup to hold my water actually helps the commons—win-win. Sucking water out of the original cup—the cup I did not create or make—depletes the commons. Using my cranial and mechanical ability to add a second cup increases the commons.

By impounding that excess water upstream, not only do we reduce these liabilities downstream during heavy rain periods, but we also create a reserve of water that we can dispense gently and strategically during droughts. That gentle and strategic dispensing can go a long way in maintaining downstream health, not to mention enhanced soil development through biomass production.

Surface runoff is special because it represents a real time commons excess, even a commons liability. Anything that impedes surface runoff creates more commons and reduces water damage. Sucking water out of aquifers, springs, and streams, however, can often deplete the commons. While arguably it is not zero sum (i.e. an irrigated corn field in western Kansas can help maintain streams and grow biomass), these natural real-time reservoirs, when depleted, represent a real time reduction in the commons.

Man-made reticulation, however, whether it's a rain barrel or a large irrigation pond catching surface runoff, represents additional water volume in the whole system. These catchments also encourage bio-active water rather than sterile water. Pond water is warmer than aquifer water, more like the temperature of rain, and therefore healthier for plants.

Just imagine if every house in your city caught all of its roof run-off in a cistern to dispense into gardens and edible landscaping during dry times. Not only could stormwater runoff systems be downsized, but it would create a veritable urban biomass bloom that would add beauty and air freshening (via transpiration and oxygenation). How about that?

If all the money spent on Los Alamos in New Mexico had been spent building surface runoff impoundments in the valleys throughout that desert region, by now the state would be an oasis of green soil development. You see, the tragedy is not that we're lazy or uncreative; the tragedy is that we're busy about the wrong things and creative on agendas that don't heal the earth. For the record, this discussion is about impoundments high on the landscape and small scale, not massive river dams.

Today, if California would embark on a massive surface runoff elimination strategy, it would have plenty of water for the down cycles. Rather than criminalizing and demonizing ponds and rain barrels as hoarding, we need to encourage these strategic interference measures as essential landscape hydration protocols. Oh, one of Yeomans' other axioms: never end a drought with a full pond. He saw water as an abundant resource to be saved and spent depending on the current climatic conditions.

In a time of ever-changing weather patterns, regardless of cause, hydrating landscapes should be a goal not only for our individual resilience, but also for our cultural commons' abundance. Both can win at this game, so let's get started. Playing with raindrops provides life-long and eco-changing entertainment.

4

Scalable

written in 2015

Those of us dedicated to regenerative agriculture have certain ideas about how to define it, or what it looks like. We usually say things like soil building, water enhancing, air cleansing, people-respecting, nutrient-enhancing, and animal honoring. These are all great litmus tests for what earth-friendly agriculture looks like.

But I'd like to add another idea to the mix: scalable. Some 25 years ago (goodness, has it been that long?) when sustainable farming folks began asking me to speak at their conferences, I'd finish with my song and dance only to hear the question: "That's fine and dandy, Joel, but does it scale up?"

It was a fair question inasmuch as at that time our farm was only a hundred acres of open land and we were servicing about 200 families with our pastured animal products. Our family was the complete and only labor force. We didn't make any deliveries, serviced no restaurants, and required customers to order in advance and drive out to the farm for scheduled pickups.

It was quaint, family-scale, highly profitable, and more fun than we could ever imagine. A lot of work, yes, but it was noble, sacred, family-centric work. Today when I finish a presentation, more often than not the first question is: "That's fine and dandy, Joel, but does it scale down?"

What happened during those 25 years that changed the question? Our farm grew, that's what happened. Today, we lease nine properties, manage 1,200 acres of open land, and figured out how to graze pigs on acorns and other goodies in the forest, which leverages another 800 acres. With staff including delivery, marketers, apprentice managers, accountants, subcontractors, apprentices, interns, and office workers, our 20-person team services 5,000 families, 50 restaurants, and 10 retail outlets.

This is not to brag, but simply to explain why the question changed. We're running nearly 1,000 head of cattle, nearly 1,000 hogs, 4,000 laying hens, 25,000 broilers and nearly 2,000 turkeys. We didn't envision this. We never had a business plan. It just happened.

But now that we're here, and the question is being asked by beginners and smaller acreage folks, it's made me ponder the whole matter of scale and I've concluded that scalability is a benchmark of correct agricultural prototypes. The beauty of our farm growth is that it has required almost no borrowed money and the infrastructure is still worthless.

Let me explain. My first eggmobile (portable laying hen house) was 6 ft. X 8 ft. by 3 ft. high mounted on bicycle wheels and housed 50 birds. I built it out of scrap for perhaps a total investment of $100. It was light enough to push around by hand. Electrified poultry netting had not yet been invented, so I built 4 ft. high and 10 ft. long poultry netting panels out of quarter-inch steel rod. Two triplicate sets allowed me to set them up like a hexagon and they stood upright due to the bends.

It worked so well that I retrofitted it the next year to mount on the tractor 3-point hitch. That way I could run them behind the cattle and let them free range. The birds tore into the cow manure, spreading out the patties and eating all the fly larvae. I knew I was onto something.

Because hooking it up to the 3-point hitch was laborious, the next year I built a bigger one 12 ft. X 20 ft. X 6 ft. high mounted on a mobile home axle. With 100 birds in there, I thought I had arrived at the big leagues. Realizing that the cost was in going out with the tractor to move it, and going out in the evening to collect the eggs, I decided to increase the numbers the next year. Besides, customers loved the eggs and asked for more.

Today, we run these eggmobiles with 400 birds apiece, in pairs hooked together, creating flocks of 800 birds. We have 6 pairs of these eggmobiles. Some are not quite as big--8 ft. X 16 ft. X 6 ft. high with 250 birds apiece, making a flock size of 500. Some of the farms we lease do not have gates big enough to accommodate the wider eggmobiles.

What's the point? Simply this: the model was profitable as a tiny backyard prototype because the infrastructure didn't cost anything. The idea could scale up with cash flow from the enterprise because the subsequently larger-sized eggmobiles were also cheap and could be added as our market grew. We didn't need to build the whole fleet in a day. We could add eggmobiles as our skill and the market expanded.

Consider the industrial alternative. If I wanted to raise eggs for the commodity market, a single egg would require a million-dollar confinement factory house. Forget the animal welfare issues, odors, or anything else. The industrial model carries an enormous entry-level price tag, which prohibits entry by almost everyone. Industrial models don't scale down easily if at all. That's why these start-ups feel compelled to grow inordinately fast and require massive infusions of venture capital. They can't start small.

If a production model is efficient or functional only at a large scale, it excludes entry-level, low-capital beginners. I would call it exclusive, or even elitist. A good model is an everyman model, or what I refer to as a "whosoever will may come" model.

On the other hand, if a production model functions well only at tiny scale, it loses credibility as a viable business and can't feed the world. While spare-time production is wonderful, limiting a model to this scale dooms it to the periphery of agricultural systems. Although I'm a big fan of tiny, and lots of tiny producers can add up to serious volume, we desperately need systems that can offer full-time salaries and feed many families.

Scalability must be seamless both up and down in order to satisfy world hunger and at the same time accept any participant. Here are some commonalities among these scalable systems.

1. Portable infrastructure. This includes shelter, water, and control (electric fence) as well as equipment. Portable systems tend to be cheap. They also divorce the farm from the land since they can be placed anywhere, whether the land is owned by the farmer or not. Eliminating land capitalization goes a long way toward enabling entry into farming. This flexibility allows more farmer-to-farmer collaboration.

2. Do-it-yourself infrastructure. Minimal construction, fabrication, and welding skills can change an otherwise capital-intensive project into a low-budget alternative. The difference in up-front costs can make or break the profitability.

3. Additional units rather than bigger stationary buildings. We all know that bigger buildings are cheaper per square foot than small ones. That pushes us to build bigger than necessary on the front end. If expansion can come from additional units rather than bigger units, building bigger at first loses its economic appeal. Rather than thinking about how big you can build something, think how small it can be and remain viable in function and profit. If one unit works, build more units.

4. Multi-purpose infrastructure. If you have to buy a machine or build a stationary building, make sure it can serve many functions. Never buy or build a single-use structure. Get more implements for the tractor, not dedicated single-function machines.

5. Use it. Don't let a machine or building sit empty or idle. Depreciation goes on whether it's used or not. If you own it, use it. Rent as long as possible. Own as a last resort, and only when you have enough volume to justify the expense. Farmer neighbors work cheap--they're used to not making any money anyway.

Scale is a real and complex issue in any discussion involving proper agriculture models. I would suggest that any model which moves seamlessly from small to large and large to small indicates integrity. Yet another benchmark of truth.

5

Downscaling Grazing
written in 2015

Many years ago when our farm had a handful of cows and a couple dozen chickens, the most frequent comment was: "That's cute, but does it scale up?" I'm convinced that one of the ways we know that our models are right is that they can scale both directions: up or down.

Today, our farm has hundreds of cows and pigs and thousands of chickens, and our pastured models work just as well. Over the years, and we've scaled them up with cash flow from retained profits. Many times a micro-farmer looks at things like portable poultry and rotational livestock grazing as something that's important for commercial operations, but not really applicable for a glorified back yard.

Nothing could be further from the truth. In this column, I want to address the homestead counterpart to our farm's commercial-scale rotations. In many ways, it's actually easier for small enterprises than larger ones.

Two overriding principles drive all others:
1. Bare soil is not good.
2. Strategically timed pruning stimulates plants.

Few things make my head explode faster than visiting a small farm and seeing a stationary chicken house surrounded by bare soil. The proverbial dirt chicken yard is not a healthy thing, no matter how small. Removing the soil's vegetative cover makes it vulnerable to erosion and shuts down biological activity.

The biological activity is important because that community of beings—from earthworms to mycorrhiza—actively working symbiotically protects pathogens from gaining the upper hand. Believe it or not, the microscopic community has far more good bugs than bad bugs. A healthy, covered, biologically active soil ensures plenty of good bugs.

If you have a postage stamp chicken yard, covering the soil with wood chips, leaves, straw or compost can ameliorate the lack of vegetation and create a living medium without green plants. I saw an interesting permutation in Canada where a fellow put 2X4s edgeways on the ground on about 1-foot centers out about 12 feet from the chicken house. The chicken doors, of course, created a high impact zone and even in a totally free-range situation, will produce barrenness over time.

He spread mesh wire over these edged boards to protect the ground. The eaves of the house dripped dew and rain water on this high impact zone where the chickens also concentrated manure (they like to poop as they enter and exit their quarters). Luxuriant green grass grew up to the wire mesh (4 inches high) and the chickens kept it mowed off perfectly. What would otherwise be a toxic, pathogen-friendly high impact zone turned instead into a productive salad bar that looked like a beautiful green carpet. Separating the chickens from the ground by a mere 4 inches completely changed the hygiene of the environment. It actually built soil instead of letting it erode.

Very cool.

Of course, anything bigger than a postage stamp can enjoy either a composting yard (lots of carbon bedding to cover the soil and let the chickens stir) or a portable structure. Whether you make one or buy one, the idea is that by leaving the birds in one place for only a day protects and maintains the vegetation. The chickens enjoy the benefit of eating fresh green material (salad bar) without destroying it.

The pruned vegetation, just like a mowed lawn, grows back quickly as soon as it's rested. Since vegetation grows in an S curve, quick pruning followed by long rest periods stimulates more biomass production than occurs in a static state. Even better than a lawn mower, the chickens leave behind fertilizer to encourage regrowth. It's win-win.

With larger flocks, lightweight electrified poultry netting offers control to gain the same win-win relationships. The whole secret to forage management is pruning and then rest. Continuous animal access to any place will eventually diminish forage production of palatable plants. All animals have a palatability index—they like ice cream better than garbanzo beans too.

Many people with a two acre lot and one dairy cow ask me: "But do I really need to rotate my cow?" The answer is yes. The first day that cow is in that 2-acre lot, she will eat the most palatable, delectable plant out there. As soon as it grows back enough for her mouth to grab, she'll bite it again. Andre Voisin, godfather of managed grazing, called this "the law of the second bite."

The whole goal of proper forage management is to protect plants from that second bite. After being pruned, the plants need enough time to go through their S growth curve—slow start, rapid acceleration, then senescent slow-down. Just to help people visualize this, I call these three stages diaper, teenage, and nursing home. If your cow continuously grazes an area, the least palatable plants will mature to nursing home status.

The most palatable plants will never get out of diaper stage. Over time, the plants the cow likes will weaken and the ones the cow doesn't like will strengthen. That's why in any continuously grazed area, regardless of climate, animal type, or plant type, the diversity of the vegetation decreases. This is why strategic timing is the key to forage management.

The timing part of the equation includes both entry and exit. In other words, it's as important when you give the animal access to a spot, called a paddock by aficionados, as it is when you exclude access. Essentially, maintaining a healthy pasture is all about managing the grazing time. That management depends on timing the forage-animal union. When we shorten the access time to eliminate the second bite, the pruning actually stimulates the forage, restarting the rapid teenage growth cycle. Without the pruning, the plant matures, turns brown, and goes dormant.

What does this look like with one milk cow? It looks like a tiny paddock offered every day. Yes, it might be only 5 yards by 10 yards (50 square yards). If you have one acre, it would offer 100 of these paddocks. That would give 99 days of rest between grazings. The rest period, of course, changes based on weather—climate, rainfall, temperature, day length. Fertility and type of vegetation also play a role. If your cow needs 50 square yards a day and you want to move her once a week, she'd get a paddock 350 square yards. But you won't get as much benefit as shorter stays. Fast-growth grass can be re-grazable in just 2 days, but that is not enough time for the plant to replenish carbohydrates expended in sending forth new shoots.

Of course, all of these paddocks are not built at one time. The fences are portable electric, enabling the grazier to adjust them as forage volume and grazing requirements change. Portable electric fence is certainly the high tech aha! of managed grazing.

The bottom line is to protect the forage from the second bite and release it immediately to a fast-growth rest period. The result is far more forage produced, far more solar energy converted into biomass, more forage diversity, and more soil organic matter developed through larger root mass.

This kind of management requires portable water and usually portable shade. Again, if you're carrying a bucket of water to a trough every day, a high impact zone occurs. Bare soil and concentrated manure—both bad and ultimately ecological losers, not to mention pathogen incubators. A simple water line supplying a float valve in a tub is cheap and worth the investment.

Simple shademobiles using nursery shade cloth will keep the animal away from trees—more high impact zones with bare soil and pathogen incubation—and spread the valuable droppings where they can be metabolized by the vegetation. When we domesticate animals on defined property, our responsibility is to figure out how to mimic the way migratory flocks and herds interacted with the landscape.

Fortunately, we have inexpensive, lightweight, portable electric fence, shelters, and water pipe that enable us, for the first time in history, to be able to duplicate domestically what occurs in natural migrations. What an incredible time to be alive. Exercising this level of management and care may sound arduous, but in the end, it's not. When you consider animal health, soil fertility, and overall pasture productivity, the dividends are wonderful. Now start movin' 'em.

Farm Policy Letter

written in 2015

We live in a sound bite era. Bombarded with information, we need to make quick judgments and move on. Nowhere is this more apparent than in the political arena. The sheer volume of words submitted for legislation precludes elected representatives from actually reading laws before voting on them.

Several years ago a Virginia delegate asked me to accompany him on a lobbying effort in the General Assembly building. That an elected official considered me an asset and not a liability was a distinct honor, so I jumped at the opportunity. He and I—just the two of us—spent the whole day going to selected offices talking with legislators.

Every time we could actually get 10-15 minutes with the senator or delegate, we received good vibes. If the legislator was too busy to see us for more than a minute, we couldn't make any headway. Of course, we couldn't begin to get around to everyone. At the end of the day, I commented to him that if we could have half an hour with each person in that building, our bill would pass. It was a bill to exempt direct farmer-to-consumer food from government licensing.

Shaking his head, the delegate gave me a piece of wisdom I've never forgotten. He said that's not how the system works. He went on to tell me that the system is designed to prohibit meaningful conversation. The hectic pace and frenetic hearings demand that politicians make up their minds quickly. "This building does not encourage thoughtful contemplation—that takes too much time. It's all about figuring out as quickly as possible which side you're on so you can go on to the next bill," he said.

I've never forgotten that lesson. From time to time, though, you and I do have moments with policy makers. We might have a few minutes or even more. In order to leverage that precious time we may have, I'd like to share some ideas for sound biting an earth stewardship and integrity food message. Essentially, if I could have 10 minutes with every elected official, here's what I'd say.

1. Nature is more powerful than you. Too often these scions we elect have an inordinate view of their own dominion. They think they can feed everyone, clothe everyone, give everyone an education, make it rain, make businesses profitable, make jobs— basically, be a fairy godmother.

The rules of nature trump Wall Street, the White House, Congress, even the Pentagon. Try as they might, all the legal posturing of the attorney general and all the military muscle of the national guard cannot build soil out of chemical fertilizer. Nature runs on carbon; it always has and it always will. It is an immutable law that demands solar power converted through photosynthesis into biomass into decomposition (digestion is one form) into food for soil beings.

Nature respects no political party, no lobbyist, no media

headlines. Nature runs on carbon, not petroleum and synthetic chemicals. Every ecosystem has animals. They aren't in factories and they don't do drugs. Nature demands multi-speciation, integration, diversity, complexity, and relational symbiosis.

We're not divine; we're dependent. We should practice more humility and less hubris. We should be caressers of the earth, not Conquistadors.

Every policy should start with a simple benchmark: does this encourage earthworms? Does this encourage soil building? No civilization can be successful when it disregards nature's rules.

2. Freedom and innovation require protecting the lunatic fringe. We know that innovation comes from those who dare to question status quo orthodoxy. Strong societies embrace whackos, knowing that the fringe doesn't jeopardize overall stability. Only fragile, fearful, failing cultures tyrannize the innovative edges with regulations, licensing, and bureaucracy.

Only a paranoid, weak civilization fears the few heretics who dare to imbibe raw milk or compost-grown tomatoes. If a deer wanders through my garden and poops next to my swiss chard, I eat it anyway as part of my immunological exercise. I want my kids to eat a pound of dirt while they grow up. That's heresy in a world of microbial soap dispensers and illegal cider sales.

Backyard chickens, home-made cheese, cottage-based charcuterie—these incubate antidotes to factory farming diseases and abuses. Farmstead and homestead self-reliance blesses society with tinkerers and odd-balls that generate tomorrow's breakthroughs. We must be free to build houses out of straw, live in teepees, experiment with herbal remedies, and engage in unsanctioned behavior like home schooling, home butchery, and home craft without bureaucrats demanding licenses, zoning permits, and infrastructure compliance.

Freedom is not academic; it is visceral. It must be tasted, touched, smelled, and seen in order to be real. So ask this question about your policy: does it increase freedom or limit it?

3. Experts are usually wrong. Politicians rely on experts, but these experts are steeped in the orthodoxy of the day. I remember well a few years ago testifying before the Virginia Senate Agriculture committee with the state's Commissioner of Agriculture. A group of us had put forward a bill to allow the sale of raw milk. The commissioner, who grew up on a dairy, said he drank raw milk religiously until he went to college and learned how dangerous it was. Then he quit drinking it.

Now, he advised the senators, not only should you not drink it, but you should make it illegal for anyone else to drink it. He was wrong, of course. On another occasion, his undersecretary said consumers were too ignorant to choose what foods to eat.

Readers of *Mother Earth News*, I would suggest, are far more knowledgeable about safe foods than these bureaucrats. We didn't buy into the hydrogenated oil agenda of the experts. We didn't buy into the margarine myth. We didn't buy into Wonder Bread as the nutritional base on the government's food pyramid. We didn't abandon our kitchens for TV dinners and processed food-like substances.

The expert media folks miss the most newsworthy occurrences of the day. The expert financial folks don't know what stock will go up or down, or who will innovate tomorrow's next great thing. Education experts today think everyone is supposed to go to college and completely miss the reality that half of humanity likes to physically work at crafts. Nutritional experts don't promote the superiority of pastured eggs or compost-grown tomatoes—they tout generic USDA labels as truth. Credentialed agriculture experts see herbicides as a weed cure and pharmaceuticals as a disease cure. All of these positions are wrong.

Here's the question: on this policy, have you heard from the peasants? Have you sought counsel from non-experts?

4. Modern economic health calculations are absurd. Our techno-sophisticated culture measures economic health based on Gross Domestic Product (GDP). That means if we have more criminals and build more jails, GDP goes up.

If we have more drug addicts and need more rehab centers for them, that's positive economic activity. The idea that all of our ills, and the costs associated with those ills, go on our balance sheets as positive economic activity is absolutely crazy.

But beyond that, we do not subtract externalized costs. Soil erosion, polluted water, and nutrient deficient food never show up on the negative side of the country's balance sheet. Collateral damage like autism, Type II diabetes, and childhood leukemia aren't negative economic figures. In fact, they're positive due to the economic activity their remediation requires. Folks, this is absurd.

The policy question is what does it do to the common wealth? Does the policy add or detract from the commons, and does it actually heal or hurt? Ultimately, if it's not healing, it's not acceptable.

There you have it. Oh, I'd like to say a whole lot more things. Goodness, I'm just getting warmed up. But we seldom have the luxury of a dissertation. As a result, a pithy, philosophically-consistent sound-bite explanation for our tribe's vision can actually touch the heart. That's a good target.

7

Debt-Limited Living
written in 2015

In light of our modern love affair with fast growth, fast money, and accelerated wealth accumulation, I'd like to propose embracing the opposite. A common business axiom is that financial collapse usually does not indicate poor product, poor marketing, or poor service. Normally, it's a cash flow crunch.

Growing businesses are always strapped for cash because accelerated sales require accelerated infrastructure and labor, which must be paid for faster than the growth can finance. The accounts payable stack up faster than the accounts receivable and before you know it, the business is out of money. Hence the insatiable quest for capital.

My own farming trajectory parallels a slow growth and limited debt path. I'm nearly 60 years old; I started my first chicken enterprise when I was 10. When Teresa (my wife) and I look at our farm sales today, our staff, our infrastructure, and our expenses, we sometimes shake our heads and ask each other: "How did we get here?" We never planned or even expected to be at our current scale; it happened largely without debt and it developed so slowly for the most part we didn't even realize where the trajectory was headed.

You could say it snuck up on us . . . over 50 years. If you stay with a plan, and keep refining it, and keep doing it, and it works, in 50 years it will develop into something. Fast money or easy money, given or borrowed, can doom anybody. Nothing stimulates creativity and motivation like being poor and hungry. We were both and I'm grateful.

But we weren't poor in character. We both came from frugal families who always lived a little below their means. If every generation lives a little below their means, wealth accumulates. My dad and mom worked off the farm in order to pay for it. When Teresa and I married, we leveraged that land into a going concern.

But we each brought some savings into the marriage, worked off farm for a couple of years, until we had enough to live on for a year. How did we accumulate those savings on modest salaries? We drove a $50 car. We remodeled the attic of the farmhouse into an apartment; we called it the penthouse. If we didn't grow it we didn't eat it. We cut our own firewood. We never went out to eat, to movies, on vacations, and didn't even have a television.

A cook out at the farm pond is as relaxing and recreational as anything money can buy. And it's a lot cheaper. I helped neighbors build fence, plant trees, make hay. Some bartered labor and others paid cash. When you're living on $300 a month, $600 goes a long way. I guarantee you that today we are leveraging those frugal years because we didn't saddle ourselves with debt. By cutting back on living expenses, we didn't have to earn much from the farm.

Sept. 24, 1982 I walked out of the newspaper office and became a full-time farmer. I was 25 years old and nobody thought we'd be successful. But we knew that as cheaply as we were living, we could survive for at least a year even if the farm didn't work out.

It was tight. We didn't know if we would make it, but somehow the pennies added up. Teresa canned and froze our garden bounty. Meals were simple, seasonal, and substantial. We never went hungry because we grew our own food.

We immediately developed a market base of families in the community who wanted pastured meat and poultry. By direct marketing, we wore all the hats of producer, processor, and marketer. We could set our prices rather than cast our wares on the commodity table.

Advertising is expensive and often risky: right target, right message? We opted for relationships. I put together a slide program about ecological pastured livestock production and presented it to dozens of civic clubs in the area. We gave samples to prospective buyers. And we rewarded word-of-mouth evangelists with free product.

All of this meant we grew slowly, but it also kept us from poor spending. If we had borrowed to grow quickly, we would not have had the experience to maintain production integrity. I've known numerous farmers who grew faster than their expertise, only to collapse when disease or sickness hit. If you can't market one pig, you can't market a dozen.

Going from 50 laying hens to 3,000 entails far more skill and management. If you aren't successful with a small number, you won't be successful with a large number. If you're struggling to keep ahead of the chores on a small place, the problems will only compound if you expend.

The problem with debt is that it enables business to grow faster than their skill level. Suddenly the operator is confronted with infrastructure limitations, knowledge inadequacy, and experience shortfalls. At that very time, the cash overheads (like debt payments) escalate and the squeeze creates a death spiral.

I encourage aspiring farmers to live in a teepee if necessary in order to stay out of debt and put every spare penny into the farm. Build a profitable farm business first. Do it on rented land. Do it on a small scale. If you only have two acres, fill it before thinking about trading to a bigger acreage.

In most areas, two acres is enough for 500 laying hens, a milk cow or two, 30 honeybee hives, 500 broilers, 50 turkeys, $20,000 worth of vegetables and specialty fruits like blackberries, raspberries, and strawberries. Jean-Martin Fortier in Quebec is leading the way showing that you can make $120,000 on less than two acres.

In my experience, size is almost never the weak link keeping a small farming enterprise from being successful. The problem is constipation of imagination. It's lack of creativity, lack of efficiency, and lack of business acumen. Fast growth will not fix any of these problems; it only compounds them.

If I can't successfully birth five calves, having a hundred to birth will not suddenly make me successful. If I can't manage my own time, having more people to manage won't help.

Every skill requires a learning curve. According to business guru Peter Drucker, that curve bottoms out around year five before climbing to success. In that valley, too many people either seek fast money or simply quit. I would suggest it is far more practical and doable to simply persevere another year, leverage your mistakes and experience, and climb out the other side without being enslaved to big debt payments.

Impatience is not only costly; it's deadly for small businesses. Enjoy the time it takes to develop skills and relational acumen. And realize that sometimes this is a multi-generational thing. You might not be able to accomplish your goals in your lifetime. That's okay. Mentor someone who will take the vision and proceed, methodically and systematically. I've heard that if your vision can be accomplished in your lifetime, it's too small.

Through the years, we've received gifts and loans from grateful customers. We've borrowed strategically when the payback was quick and assured. Deferred growth is much sweeter than immediate debt payments. You never have to repay a loan you didn't accept. If you want more, then be creative enough to figure out how to make it happen without saddling yourself with a burdensome debt. Debt is a hard taskmaster.

My dad used to say: "We make haste slowly." Allan Nation, editor of *Stockman Grass Farmer* magazine, says: "Profitable farms always have a threadbare look." When you visit our farm, you won't see fancy fences, spiffy buildings, or expensive landscaping. We use what we have, for as long as we can, as frugally as possible. It'll never get us Wall Streetified respect, but it lets us sleep at night. And that makes us wealthy.

8

Upgrading Woodlots

written in 2015

T hat woodlot out behind the garden needs stewardship just as much as any other piece of a homestead. Too often, though, we leave the forest patch to its own devices, as if it's some sort of sacred shrine to wildness that dare not be desecrated by human intervention.

I have news for you: dense forests did not exist in North America 600 years ago. Using fire, Native Americans routinely burned the landscape to keep back dense undergrowth and maintain a more pastoral, or open look. Widely spaced trees grew better with space to spread and more nutrients to enjoy.

New discoveries about the pre-European landscape show a meticulous interaction from humans, massaging and changing plant and animal communities. By burning routinely, native-lit fires were not towering infernos of conflagration. Rather, they were what foresters today call cold fires. These more gentle fires do not jump into the tree canopy, but stay low to the ground, burning brush, brambles, and small saplings.

These cold fires killed only weak trees. The strong trees lived through these fires and became even stronger with their competition weeded out. Just like garden vegetables thrive when given plenty of room and freed from competing weeds, trees released by fire or thinning become stronger and grow more rapidly.

So if you and I could close our eyes and imagine what a routinely burned landscape looked like in 1500, we would see widely spaced trees in a savannah type setting. Few trees would be crooked, diseased, stunted or otherwise inferior. Century after century, prior to Europeans' arrival, North American forests enjoyed this fire stewardship. Here's the key point: this management killed weaklings, leaving only superior genetic stock. Over the centuries, this management upgraded tree genetics and created the magnificent cathedral specimens that early settlers described in their diaries.

In the native American silviculture economy, large, widely spaced trees were a natural result of this management. Further, their fires and buildings primarily used small diameter saplings and pole timber, again favoring widely spaced large trees. Without saws in their tool chest, these natives simply could not efficiently harvest large trees.

All of this favored what I call survivor genetics and resulted in upgraded genes in the trees that matured.

Then the Europeans arrived. These are my ancestors, so at this point I'll go to personal pronouns. For us, the big trees were the most valuable. And we had metal saws, which enabled us to not only cut large trees down, but to cut them up into usable lumber.

This reversed the multi-century—perhaps multi-millenia—management plan that favored surviving big trees. With the value skewed toward big trees, those were the first ones harvested. Today, our forests are literally centuries into the best being harvested and the poorest being left to grow.

Such a protocol over time downgrades the genetic base. No livestock farmer could imagine selecting mangy weaklings as breeding stock. No seed producer could imagine selecting seed from the weakest vegetables to plant next year. The history of ecology and agriculture is largely the chronology of genetic selection wherein the stronger ones attain to breedable status and the weaker ones die off or are killed by predators.

But when I look at our basic forest management, it's exactly the opposite. Foresters refer to this as highgrading-- taking the best and leaving the worst. The problem is we don't have a forestal or wood-based economy that incentivizes taking the worst and leaving the best. This is a major conundrum for us tree huggers—and I mean this viscerally. I'm always putting my arms around trees to estimate their girth and enjoy their strength.

But if I'm going to upgrade my woodlot, I can't continuously take these big ones; I must figure out a way to take the diseased, infirmed, crooked, and weaklings. Those occupy valuable space that could be growing genetically superior individuals. Again, a poor cow eats just as much as a good cow. Nobody would argue with a farmer who culled the poor cow and replaced it with the good cow's heifer calf. Likewise, nobody would argue the wisdom of disregarding seeds from weak vegetables.

So why do we enter our degraded, genetically inferior woodlots as if what's there is too sacred to receive the weeder's chainsaw? Most of our woodlots (I daresay all, but there might be an exception somewhere) have far more weedy, weak, and wounded trees than good ones. How do we pay ourselves for the time and effort it takes to get rid of them?

Today's forestal economy only recognizes lumber as

what's valuable. And a forestal economy built only on boardfeet will inherently experience degradation. We desperately need value for the culls so that we can begin again to fill our wood-lots with superior genetics and reverse this multi-century slide.

This brings me to the point of this column and the question with amazing ramifications: what if all the money currently spent in the U.S. on chemical fertilizer were spent instead on wood-based carbon to feed soil? To fully explore this question would take a whole book, but let me give a teaser.

If you're reading *Mother Earth News* you no doubt understand that carbon is what builds soil. This magazine is filled with tips on composting, mulching, lasagna gardens and feeding earthworms. Some 75 percent of everything that has been dumped into landfills since their inception is compostable, and that's an immoral blot on our culture, to be sure.

But if we truly moved to a carbon economy, replacing all chemical fertilizers with compost, we would need vast stores of carbon. I recently traveled through northern Colorado and was shocked to see literally millions of acres of dead trees. When I asked my hosts why they were all dead, the answer was quick and axiomatic: no diversity, too thick, no fire or cutting management.

With today's machinery, from chainsaws to chippers to tub grinders and front end loaders, wildfires should be seen as a manifestation of stewardship neglect. I submit that if we took all the money our nation spends to make sure petroleum stays cheap and readily available and invested it instead in woodlot upgrading, we'd have far healthier soil and a far healthier economy. Other countries might even start to like us again.

Last winter we hired a Vermeer chipper that could handle 19 inch diameter material. In two days we cleared an acre of old dying Virginia pine, converting it to four tractor trailer loads of carbon that we used to bed our cattle, chickens and pigs during the winter. Turning that into compost, we hauled all that material onto our fields in the spring, covering literally fifty acres.

Now dear folks, if one acre of dying forest can cover fifty acres with compost, imagine what that could do as a national policy. We'd have thousands of jobs—domestic jobs—employing people on the landscape, not in Dilbert cubicles chasing fantasy numbers around cyberspace. Real work for real people on real land doing real meaningful management.

And can you imagine the dancing earthworms if such a scheme took hold? Instead of running from toxic chemicals, they'd be feasting on compost, aerating, mineralizing, and loosening the soil.

Wood pellet technology is fast approaching the do-it-yourself level, offering yet another economic enterprise for low quality forestry products. Gasification, rocket stoves, wood-fired steam engines. Goodness, with all this new technology we could actually create an economically viable forestry upgrade program. I can imagine an entire tree-weeding industry replacing our current military-based petroleum-centric chemical fertilizer program.

I would suggest that this idea is not a cap-and-trade scheme, not a contrived carbon-trading Wall Street plan, but rather a protocol as old as nature itself. Indeed, it honors and relies on the oldest tried-and-true earth stewardship pattern we know: the carbon cycle. That's something all of us can embrace.

9

Death & Children

written in 2015

For a couple of years now David Schaefer of Featherman Plucker fame and I have been doing a chicken processing demonstration at *The Mother Earth News* fairs. To set the context, this is the real deal: we actually kill, scald, pluck, eviscerate, and chill eight pastured chickens. We do our best not to leave anything to the imagination.

This year, for the first time, an innocent 9-year-old attendee asked to come up on stage with us and before I knew it, he pulled off a chicken head, raised it triumphantly and the crowd clapped and hooted. Before David and I could collect ourselves, other children came up, some peering into the scald water, others grabbing a souvenir foot, and others trying their hand at pulling off heads.

At each child's success, the crowd clapped. Although this is a serious how-to workshop, only one of dozens offered at each fair (if you haven't been to one, go: it's the experience of a lifetime), it goes better with a few theatrics. David and I looked at each other and realized we had definitely opened a new dimension of theatrics to our otherwise hard core session.

While the response is overwhelmingly positive, some folks

are aghast at the notion of letting children actively participate in this exercise. In this column, I'd like to tackle this thorny issue a bit.

I think the tension is comprised of two parts. The first part is the overarching notion that eating meat is unnecessary and immoral, that killing sentient beings is uncivilized and uncharitable. Related notions include domestic livestock destroys the planet and eating meat decreases health. Animals are meant to photograph, pet, and play. Ideally, all animals would have a monogrammed L.L. Bean lounge pillow in climate-controlled ante-rooms. What a life.

Dear folks, such a notion does not indicate a new state of evolutionary cosmic awareness; rather, it indicates a devolutionary state of profound disconnectedness to the life-death-decomposition-regeneration choreography that underpins all life on the earth. Everything is eating and being eaten; if you don't believe it, go lie naked in your flower bed for three days and see what gets eaten.

When a maple tree withholds sap during a wind storm to preserve its precious cleansing fluid (blood) lest a broken branch make a large wound, that's sentient. When the leaves change their chemical composition to become less tasty to munching herbivores and bugs, that's sentient. All of nature is pulsing with observation, language, and adaptation. We know that the three custodial bacteria guarding every human cell talk to each other. This is sentient. A compost pile, perhaps better than anything, illustrates this biological cycle that requires death in order to live.

If we assume that death is part of life, that animal slaughter epitomizes what goes on every day in the soil and in our bodies, then the second issue involves the appropriate age for participation. I find it fascinating that this discussion did not enter the mainstream until the last couple of decades.

The idea that a person could be removed from viscerally participating in food production and processing, including slaughtering animals, is completely aberrant in human history. The Western world's luxury makes it possible to be this disconnected from our ecological umbilical. Absent that luxury, and we'd be like most places on the planet where a child would welcome a piece of chicken for dinner, or a glass of milk.

Failure to contemplate that something must be sacrificed in order that something else may live can seem like a small thing, but I submit that it profoundly affects how a person values life. And how a person views personal responsibility to the overall system that sustains life.

On our farm and in our family, we never shielded our children from the cost of life. Whether it was pulling weeds in the garden in order to grow a crop of green beans, cutting and stacking firewood so we could stay warm in the winter, or butchering chickens in order to have sustenance next week, we involved them in everything—from day one. We saw no inappropriate time to expose them to the depth and breadth, the mystery and majesty, of life's choreography.

To grow up thinking life's most serious challenge is rising to the top of Angry Birds or Panda Pop actually inhibits children. How? They don't understand the gravity of life. The preciousness of life. The repercussions of our decisions. To stare our own dependency in the face as we care for and then harvest our food shapes the mind and humbles the spirit.

It's time to take a breath. I'm sure some folks are disgusted, perhaps even violently offended, at what I've just said. "What about animal abuse, factory farms, and those awful factory slaughterhouses?" you may ask. Believe me, all of those things disgust me as much as anyone else. Scale makes a difference—may I say, a huge difference?

In our fair poultry demonstrations, David and I go to great lengths to show humane techniques for slaughter: as David says, "squawkless dispatch." It is primarily a Kosher or Halal protocol, which I for one feel good to have on my side.

Perhaps we can eliminate the factory farms and processing facilities if we train up our children to be self-reliant and enjoy participating in their food system. That such horrible large-scale operations exist testifies not to our efficiency, but to our assumption that integrity can exist in a climate of ignorance. That so few people know how their animals are handled—on the farm or anywhere else—gives place for abuse to exist.

I would go so far as to suggest that modern slaughterhouses are inhumane to the humans who work there. Nobody should kill animals every day. And in this column, while I'm encouraging children to participate in the process, by no means do I advocate anyone slaughtering animals every day. That creates callousness and probably does move us toward emotional imbalance.

But when the person who cares for the animal participates in its final use, that sacrifice takes on a sacredness rather than sacrilege. Honoring the animal in life, by providing it a diet and living conditions in which it can express its distinctiveness (the chickenness of the chicken) elevates the harvest to a place of honor and awe.

The factory farm cannot offer a sacred sacrifice because it has demeaned and cheapened the life from day one. But when animals are raised with respect and honor, their slaughter brings us face to face with our own frailty, our dependence, and our profound responsibilities to life and stewardship. It is never too early for children to face these issues.

Having helped children slaughter chickens for decades, I believe exposure needs to happen prior to 10 years old. If it hasn't by then, more often than not the first experience evokes ishy-gishy revulsion rather than innocent embrace. Parents who accept this responsibility for their little ones, but who have never seen it, often wrestle more with the experience than their children.

The open-hearted and discovery-oriented mind and spirit of children make a slaughter event part of their life awareness. Adults who have been disconnected from this all their lives get knots in their stomachs. Festivals and food go together. Bringing that food from field to festive table is not supposed to be something that turns our emotions into knots.

Slaughtering animals is the final homage we pay to our care and stewardship, where we actually take into our bones and cells the being we've protected, fed, and watered. That is intimacy taken to a new level. Encouraging our children to understand, to witness, to participate in that kind of relationship actually builds loyalty and character. I would argue that denying our children that grounding in what life ultimately requires opens them up to me-centeredness and shallow thinking.

If the life is raised well, harvested well, eaten with gratitude, nothing about that beautiful cycle can impair the spirit or emotions. That beauty entails some disturbance, just like chisels on a diamond. But as long as the difficult times create the beautiful, our children will get the whole picture, and they'll be balanced emotionally and spiritually.

10

Earthworms

written in 2016

What fascinates you? What occupies your fixation?
At the risk of being dismissed as certifiably weird,
may I humbly submit the earthworm as deserving
both our fixation and fascination.

When my parents purchased this farmland in 1961,
the soil was thin, infertile, and completely unproductive.
Earthworms did not exist. Today, literally inches of new top soil
support vibrant production and copious earthworm populations.

In many ways, earthworms are a litmus test for soil
fertility. Anyone farming or gardening needs to be both fixated
and fascinated by this fertility facilitator. All of the icons in
the sustainability movement have been students of the lowly
earthworm—Sir Albert Howard, Rodale, Mollison.

Howard wrote: "They [earthworms] are the ideal soil
analysts and furnish the gardener with a report on the state of
his land far more instructive than anything the soil scientist has
so far provided. All that is necessary is for the gardener himself
to make a rough count of the earthworms in the top spit of soil
and to observe their color, general condition and above all their
liveliness. If, in each spadeful during the autumn digging, one

glistening, red, active lob-worm occurs, about the thickness of a man's little finger, then all is well with the soil and quality of next season's crop is assured."

Father of modern composting and arguably foundational practitioner of scientific sustainable agriculture, Howard pointed out that earthworm tunnels provide ventilation for air and water to penetrate into the soil. Secondly, he said earthworms "condition the food materials needed by the roots of plants."

An earthworm is a sightless creature with a gizzard, three calciferous glands, an alimentary canal, and made in rings surrounded by bristles. According to *Rodale's Complete Book of Composting*, earthworms do not move by zigzagging like a snake. Rather, they compress and expand with their rings and bristles, moving straight through the soil.

Most people think ants are strong for their size, but earthworms are arguably the ultimate strength creature. Weighing only 1/30th of an ounce, they routinely move 2 ounce stones, equivalent to a 150-pound person moving a 9,000 pound stone.

What I find most amazing about earthworms, and indeed still baffles scientists, is that the castings coming out of the alimentary canal contain 5 times the nitrogen (N), 7 times the phosphorous (P) and 11 times the potash (K) of the soil context in which the worm lives. It's almost like alchemy because no net loss occurs. This is not taking a lot and excreting a little. This is simply recombining—what Howard called "conditioning"—vegetable matter and minerals into a perfect fertility capsule.

In addition, the alimentary canal detoxifies the material entering, offering a truly clean, pathogen-free casting out the back end. Earthworm castings are the magic elixir coveted by good gardeners and farmers throughout the world. Depending on what researcher you read, a healthy earthworm population can create from half an inch to an inch of fertile topsoil every 5 years. This is no small feat.

At the beginning of this column, I mentioned that as a young boy, I couldn't find an earthworm on our farm. Now, as a much older boy (ha!), I have to be careful how I walk across the fields to keep from turning my ankle on the earthworm casting mounds. Okay, that may be a bit extreme, but we literally have 2-inch tall mounds everywhere. Indeed, we've had visitors bring recording equipment to capture the sound of earthworms retreating into their tunnels as you walk along.

What changed? How do you attract these healers of the earth, builders of soil? We never bought earthworms or inoculated our fields with earthworm eggs. Few beings are as resilient as earthworms. Both they and their eggs can lie dormant for a long time—perhaps years—when conditions are inhospitable. Then when conditions change, they can come to life, hatch, and be productive.

Folks who study earthworms agree on several key elements. First, earthworms thrive in cool, dark, damp conditions. They prefer a Goldilocks environment: not too hot, not too cold; just right. Denuded soil is the quickest way to destroy healthy earthworm populations.

That can be caused either by clean tillage, dirt chicken yards, or overgrazing. Vegetation is the protective covering of the earth; naked earth is like a wound to nature. Seeds, carried on the wind, feathers, hides of animals, and lying dormant in the soil, are an insurance policy against earth nakedness.

Have you ever moved an old board lying undisturbed for months, only to discover a dozen fat, beautiful earthworms lying underneath? The board protects the soil from drying out and ensures a dark, cool environment. Drawn to this environment, the worms set up housekeeping and perform their magic.

This is why mulching, whether with vegetable material or black plastic, encourages earthworm activity. It's also why deep, lush pastures created by rotational grazing stimulate earthworms. If you have a lot where a horse, cow, goat, chicken—name your critter—stays all the time and keeps the vegetation pruned to ground level, the earthworms will leave or go dormant, or both. By allowing the forage to grow to its phenotypical zenith, or full expression, the dense canopy acts as a mulch to cool down, darken, and moisten the soil.

Some of the most abused land in the world is not under corn and soybeans, but in backyard lots where daily animal impaction hardens the soil and denudes it of vegetative cover. If we're actually going to heal land—and I believe this is our human imperative—then we must provide a habitat that encourages earthworms.

A deep vegetative cover also warms the soil during early spring and late fall when an exposed soil cools down too fast or warms up too slowly. Earthworms like things cool, but not cold. They like things damp, but neither dry nor wet. The thicker the soil canopy, whether living forage or dead carbon (wood chips, leaves, straw), the easier it is to maintain these parameters.

Secondly, manure and compost stimulate earthworm proliferation. Again, we don't know all the whys, but we do know that earthworms prefer manures and compost. This of course begs the question if a farm without animals can be a worm-friendly place. Certainly manure-based compost can be imported, as long as transportation energy remains relatively cheap.

But in the big scheme of things, nature has no animal-less ecosystems. Perhaps one reason is to feed and encourage healthy earthworm populations. It goes without saying that chemical fertilizers and the whole array of industrial additives, from pesticides to herbicides, are not conducive to earthworm activity. Some may argue that increasing vegetative growth through chemical fertilization does increase earthworm activity, and that may be true, but these acid-based nutrients are toxic to earthworms and only the additional plant growth buffers the damage being caused.

Nothing should be applied to the soil that the earthworm can't eat. And certainly anything deadly to an earthworm should not be applied. Fortunately for those of us who do large scale composting, the earthworm can take a relatively rough, or unfinished material, and finish it in the soil. Here at Polyface, we don't worry about making perfect compost that looks like potting soil. When it smells sweet and humusy, we spread it and depend on earthworm diligence to finish its conversion to root-ready goodies.

Third, earthworms like unmolested soil. Tillage not only chops up many of these partners, but it destroys their tunnels. This is why most of the best gardeners today practice either shallow tillage (Eliot Coleman), no tillage (Jean-Martin Fortier, Paul Gautschi, permaculture), or gentle deep crumbling like broadforking (John Jeavons, Eliot Coleman), or combinations of these (John Moody). The point is that deep egg-beater tillage and soil profile inversion are too disturbing to the earthworm community.

This is certainly one of the benefits of permaculture, which minimizes tillage by encouraging perennials rather than annuals. Anything we can do to decrease aggressive soil disturbance leaves the earthworm tunnels and communities intact. As my friend and sustainable entrepreneur Bill Wolf says: "Earthworms like to be fed on top of their heads." In other words, the idea that we need to aggressively till in order to place the organic matter and rocks near their accommodations is simply opposite what the earthworms want.

They burrow—sometimes as deep as 12-14 feet— vertically, bringing minerals from down deep, depositing them on top of the soil, and taking organic materials down into the soil. This industrious and meticulous activity should be encouraged with compost, manures, living and non-living covers, rather than impeded with inappropriate aggressive tillage.

I never tire of getting down on my hands and knees in lush pasture, parting the forage, and finding mountains of earthworm castings. Visitors are often astonished, having never seen casting pillars. Ultimately, a civilization's health is dependent on the health and vibrancy of its earthworms. They are more important than regulations, business, or entertainment. What am I doing, what are you doing, to insure the copious copulating choreography of the amazing earthworm?

Measuring What Isn't

written in 2016

This sounds like something out of Dr. Seuss, but it's true: it's hard to measure what isn't.

I've been noticing an accelerating and antagonistic anti-meat vibe in American media. Those of us engaged in domestic livestock production find ourselves increasingly demonized by various and sundry groups.

Of course, the most militant animal welfarists condemn us for enslaving creatures and then violently killing them. Diet dictocrats, as Sally Fallon terms them, push a vegetarian or vegan agenda as a one-size-fits-all panacea for the earth's and society's woes. Radical environmentalists pin climate change and everything resource-depleting, from water to soil to oxygen on domestic livestock.

The accusations seem more strident by the day and I find myself feeling like a punching bag. It really gained traction with the now widely debunked *The China Study*, which is still touted by vegans as scientific. Then it went into hyper-speed with the U.N. Long Shadow report, which again countless scientists have shown was nothing more than a prejudicial puff piece for the anti-animal lobby. More recently, the documentary *Cowspiracy* attacked meat eaters and livestock producers as planetary pariahs.

The snowball seems bigger and accelerating. I won't debunk these things point by point because plenty of more credentialed experts than I have done it better than I ever could. Unfortunately, these anti-meat crusades are generally correct in their data and extrapolations.

I'm sitting there watching *Cowspiracy* saying: "Amen. Preach it, brother." But in disparaging the industrial, concentrated animal feeding operation (CAFO) system, it commits the fatal flaw of witch hunters: every one who has a broom is guilty. The logic goes like this. Look at cows today. They are bad. Therefore, anyone who has a cow is bad.

It's quite simplistic, but that's the idea. Anyone who has a chicken is a Tyson monster. A pastured pig is identical to Smithfield. A grass-finished cow is the same as a feedlot bovine. What's amazing is that recently I'm even seeing environmentalists say pastured animals are worse than CAFO animals. So if you're going to eat meat, eat the CAFO industrial fare; it's better for the planet than land-wasting animals gamboling on a pasture.

It's enough to make my head explode. In one of these explosive moments, I had an epiphany that I want to share. It dawned on me that the one commonality in all this demonizing is the starting data point. Think about this. If you want to go to Grandma's house 1,000 miles away in an airplane, if you start just 1 degree wrong, you aren't going to end up at Grandma's house.

We farmers see this principle every day when we birth things. We know that the whole trajectory of the plant or animal is determined by seemingly tiny forces. Genes. Soil quality. Water. Ambient temperature (try not giving a new set of chicks the correct ambient temperature and see how many get to maturity—their equivalent of flying to Grandma's house). The point is that little things at the beginning have major influences as the journey goes along.

All of these studies start at the same place: industrial agriculture. The few who do take into account non-industrial production go clear to the other extreme and measure unmanaged systems. For example, herbivores on continuously-grazed pastures.

After cogitating on all these allegedly scientific conclusions, it struck me like a bolt of lightning: you can't study what isn't. None of these folks have come to our farm, nor any farm like ours. Indeed, when Allan Savory, originator and guru of holistic management finally received an audience with the producers of *Cowspiracy*, they couldn't have been more unresponsive.

Here's a man who has built soil, re-started long-defunct springs in arid regions, and increased biomass production exponentially—all with holistic management. And he's not the only one. Many, many livestock producers around the world have had the same success and seen the same benefits.

On our farm, we lovingly call our system mob stocking herbivorous solar conversion lignified carbon sequestration fertilization. That's a mouthful, of course, but it speaks to the many symbiotic nuances of using high-tech monitoring and infrastructure to achieve the same kind of ecological synergies as nature's choreographies. It should give us all pause to realize that there were more pounds of animals in North America 500 years ago than there are today.

That exceptional soil building, biomass-producing, hydrating ecosystem occurred without hybrids, chemical fertilizers and pesticides, or tractors. Diaries of early explorers contain accounts of bison herds 50 miles long and 20 miles wide so dense that the prairie could not be seen between the animals. Audubon, the famous naturalist/ornithologist, said he couldn't see the sun for three days because a flock of birds (presumably passenger pigeons) blocked it out. Anyone seen a flock of birds lately that blotted out the sun for three days?

Literally millions of beavers had up to 8 percent of the landscape protected with beaver ponds. Folks who study these things tell me that even in the arid southwest the number of beaver ponds was astronomical. Imagine all that water and erosion protection.

California had millions of meg-fauna. More people lived in Nebraska and Kansas 500 years ago than live there today. The empty continent found by Europeans in roughly 1600 appeared that way because 90 percent of the native population had been decimated by European diseases during the previous century. Remember, Columbus sailed the ocean blue in 1492. The point is that a lot of animal production—arguably more than we're doing today even with CAFOs—occurred for centuries prior to European conquest.

Where was the soil depletion? The desertification? The climate change? It wasn't. And it doesn't have to be today either if we duplicate the kind of principles exhibited by these early animals. Due to predators, hunting, weather, and fire, these migratory herds and flocks (don't forget millions of prairie chickens) exhibited clear patterns of moving, mobbing, and mowing.

They didn't park themselves in a field. They didn't roost in the same trees every night. And the beavers. Don't forget them. Permaculture's accent on water via pond building is truly hydration's best friend. But do these scientists condemning livestock rearing and meat eating study highly functional permaculture livestock farms? No.

The ugly truth is that the number of truly regenerative, nature-duplicating farms, with all the intricacies of pre-European systems, simply don't exist in the world of these credentialed scientists. It's such a small world that in reality, it doesn't exist. And so it's hard to study what isn't.

Extrapolating data from a flawed base is like starting that flight to Grandma's house not with a 1 percent compass deviation, but a 180 degree deviation. Can you imagine doing a study on education and using as your data base the worst classroom in the country? Could the researcher be faulted for concluding that education is not a good thing? That teachers are evil? That all schools should be shuttered. That we should grow tomorrow's students in petri dishes?

Can you imagine studying the value of religion by using the most dysfunctional church congregation as the data baseline? You'd want to abolish churches and become an atheist. Yet this is exactly what these credentialed academic research studies have done. They've measured the worst of the worst, the most dysfunctional, anti-ecological, animal-abusive, nutrient-devitalizing system conceivable and concluded that animals are bad.

Today I read a report that said animals destroy wildlife. Yes, if they're housed in feedlots and fed mono-cultured, chemically-doused grains. This past summer we had some Smithsonian scientists here on our farm studying soil, bees, birds, and plant diversity to quantify the effect of our livestock production systems. Guess what? We're off the charts! Every bumblebee known to exist in Virginia is thriving right here on our farm—along with cows, chickens, pigs, turkeys, rabbits, sheep, ducks, and some fairly rambunctious people.

And guess what they found in our soil? Carbon! Averaging 8 percent. Most farm soils in the U.S. are now down to 1 percent. We were too 50 years ago. But livestock built that soil. It sequestered that carbon. But it didn't do it with CAFOs and mono-crops and chemicals. It did it the old way—nature's tried and true system.

We force migrations around our farm with electric fence and portable shelters. We've built a dozen ponds and have installed 6 miles of water lines—eat your hearts out, beavers. But you see, dear folks, in the world of prestigious agriculture colleges and industrial food/farm fraternities, our farm and the few others like it don't exist.

We don't get invited to their dinners. We write in *The Mother Earth News*, not the magazines adorning the shelves of any self-respecting land grant university's agriculture library. We're classic outliers, completely outside the purview, awareness, and even interest of the big school orthodoxy. That's where the research money is. That's where the power, prestige, and profits are.

If farms like ours became an is instead of an isn't (how about that, Dr. Seuss) just imagine the disturbance it would create. Goodness, veterinarians would be begging for work. Doctors would be twiddling their thumbs. The 20 percent of petroleum use that goes into chemical fertilizers could stay in the ground. Maybe we wouldn't have to fight over it. Ahhh, now there's something to keep from happening.

Many of you reading *The Mother Earth News* can remember a conversion day. A day when the lights went on. It may have been a personal illness or that of a friend. Perhaps finding out what those unpronounceables on the labels actually were. But those of us who embrace nature's patterns realize that we're still a minority and for the vast majority of our culture, immersed in the Kardashians and professional sports, we're an isn't.

And that's how we get highly touted peer-reviewed hogwash. If it doesn't exist in your world, it's just not there. And you can't measure what isn't.

12

What You Can Do

written in 2016

Do you ever feel like the whole world is crazy and what can your lone voice do to change things? We're tempted to go over in a corner and have a pity party because the insanity seems overwhelming.

Let me introduce you to an Australian buddy of mine, Jack. He's seven years old and lives in the province of Queensland. His parents own a small farmstead where they practice permaculture. They make their living organizing and hosting educational seminars to acquaint farmers and ranchers in Australia with the best earth-friendly production practices available on the planet. Jack has good parents.

Jack's teacher at school incentivized a new reading initiative by handing out lollipops to the highest achievers. An extremely bright boy, Jack got his and looked it over. Growing up in an earth-aware, nutrition-interested, self-reliant family he had grave doubts that this thing in his hand was something he should indulge.

He took it home and asked his mom and dad if it was okay to eat. His dad, being a wise man and skilled in the Socratic method, responded with a simple answer: "What's

70

in it?" Why couldn't I be such a wise parent? The answer is non-judgmental, but challenges the child to seek on his own. Brilliant.

What ensued was almost an obsessive internet search for lollipop ingredients. Then he searched for health benefits or harms from those ingredients. To his horror and dismay, his own research led him to believe that lollipops contained things that could give him cancer.

A couple of days later he went to the teacher—not his parents, mind you—and said: "I don't want to eat something that will give me cancer. I don't want the lollipop." Taken aback, the judicious teacher responded: "Okay, I won't give you one."

Feeling like he scored a victory, Jack felt good. He'd stood up for his convictions and created a protective hedge for himself. That evening, though, as he contemplated what had happened, he didn't feel good about it anymore. Now mind you, he arrived at all this by himself, without parental goading.

The next day he went to the teacher (I hope all you wonderful elementary school teachers out there are enjoying this) and said: "It's okay that I don't have to eat something that might cause cancer. But these other kids are my friends, and I don't want them to get cancer." Wow. Yes, tears are fine at this point.

That afternoon, Jack's mother received a call from the school principal. By this time, the children in the class had begun to murmur. Did I mention that Jack is precocious? You probably figured that out by now, but I thought I'd better make that clear. We must also make it clear that Jack's classmates thought he was a bit wacko. But Jack had courage, conviction, and obviously a heart that wrapped itself around those classmates.

Jack's mother, calmly, offered the principal Jack's research. The next day Jack toted his printed-off research file to the principal's office. Two months later the principal issued his official ruling: "The evidence is not conclusive."

At this point, Jack's mother, like a true tigress, stepped in. She asked the principal one simple question: "Why would you risk it?" He didn't have an answer, and the next day issued his final position: "We will stop giving lollipops to our students." You can clap now.

In full disclosure, I don't believe eating one lollipop will give you cancer. I don't even think eating at McDonald's one time will kill you. It's the habit that's the problem. It's the convictionless go-with-the-flow orthodoxy that we must arrest. Jack, a seven-year-old, was not embarrassed or cowed by teachers, principals, or peer pressure. One small voice changed an entire school policy. And yes, this is a true story. When I go to Australia, Jack and I are buddies. Wouldn't you want him for your buddy?

The thing I love about this story is how it flows out one little piece at a time. Most of us are intimidated by the sheer magnitude of the things that are messed up in our country. From tax policy to foreign policy, from agriculture subsidies to monocrops and aquifer depletion, the issues are monstrous. They're complex. And it seems like more people have their hands in the pie of deficit-funded largesse than have their hands minding their own businesses and tending their own gardens.

The whole thing can be depressing and emotionally debilitating. But in his iconic book *7 Habits of Highly Effective People*, Steven Covey admonishes us to be content within our "sphere of influence." Few things disempower faster than causes too big to tackle. To be sure, some people have a pretty big stage, and a larger pond in which to create ripples.

I was interviewed for a radio show last week and the first question concerned the farm bill. What did I think—the usual stuff. I admitted I don't even know what's in it and don't read it. It's too big for me, too complicated. Nothing gets solved with the farm bill anyway. Changing the money from one group of people to another group of supposedly better recipients will only push the good guys toward corruption. Changing the corruption from Group A to Group B doesn't fundamentally change anything.

I only have 24 hours in a day, just like everyone else. What's my best return on that time? Some people are policy wonks, and thrive on signing petitions, marching, and organizing rallies. God bless 'em.

But I think a lot can be said for the notion of just opting out of the messed up system. Just quit taking the lollipops. What does that look like in the grown up world? Does it look like a bunch of hippies holding hands sitting cross-legged on the beach singing Kumbaya? Does it look like a tent city perched on the capital lawn?

You see, I'm convinced that most people who rail against the system aren't offering a visceral object lesson of a credible alternative. What does a rebel look like in our modern America? What does an adult Jack do?

Here are some ideas to get you thinking. Get in your kitchen. Do you know how much mess has been created because Americans abdicated domestic culinary responsibilities? From TV dinners to Lucky Charms, the lion's share of the entire adulterated diet is symptomatic of leaving the kitchen. Lest anyone jump to conclusions, this is not a sexist statement. When people ask: "What can we do?" my first answer—regardless of gender—is "Get in your kitchen."

Our kitchens have never been more techno-glitzy gadgetized. Let's leverage the technology to prepare, process, package and preserve whole, local, compost-grown foods in our kitchens. That would simply de-fund the food adulteration complex.

Secondly, how about grow a garden? Did you know the U.S. has 46 million acres of lawn? And we have 45 million acres housing and feeding recreational horses. That's more than enough land to feed the entire country if we adopted bio-intensive guru John Jeavons' gardening methods. Ultimate food security can never come from a warehouse; it comes from an in-house larder. How about that vacant lot next door? Turn it into an urban farm.

Thirdly, create self-reliant homesteads. Cisterns, solariums, backyard chickens. That gives our children chores to do, and that would solve half our domestic and juvenile emotional issues. Kids want to engage meaningfully in the adult world. If the only thing they can do is play video games, no wonder they grow up confused and childish. This isn't abuse; it's the greatest legacy we can imagine. Responsible, nurturing, persevering, dependable youths.

Finally, I'd suggest seeing how little you can earn rather than how much. Money, things made in China—they don't ultimately satisfy. Engaging with the earth's most visceral functions, building familial and social relationships, bettering your own character and cerebral capacity—these are way better than coins. Just ask the Kardashians. Oh, it might be alluring for a time, but sooner or later you face the brevity of life and ask about what matters.

What matters will be when your inner Jack reveals himself. Leaving a legacy of nutritious gardens and a pantry of homemade food instead of lollipops is noble, sacred, rebellious, and ultimately helpful. Now go change your world.

13

Mechanical vs. Biological

written in 2016

Is life fundamentally biological or mechanical? How you answer that question defines how you view life and in turn sets boundaries on innovation regarding life. I see this question as foundational to distinguishing between the industrial and ecological farm/food systems. I've also found that in discussions with industrial food system defenders, this question forces more head scratching than any other.

The Mother Earth News staff asked me to use this column as a bit of a teaser for my new book *The Marvelous Pigness Of Pigs: Nurturing and Caring for All God's Creation.* This book grew out of my observations that, for the most part, the faith community fails to embrace an environmental ethic that matches the menu to the pew. If all life is simply mechanical, then it's inert protoplasmic structure like plastic or clay and therefore able to be manipulated however cleverly hubris can imagine to manipulate it.

Those of you who know me know that I have purposely chosen the moniker Christian libertarian environmentalist capitalist lunatic farmer in order to humorously dispel the stereotypes that inevitably follow my ecological farming persona. To my Christian friends, I spend a lot of time apologizing for the radical anti-business, big-government, abortion-friendly stance of my environmentalist friends. To my environmentalist friends, I spend a lot of time apologizing for the corporate-industrialist, cheap food, limitless dominion, Monsanto-friendly stance of my Christian friends.

With my feet firmly planted in both of those worlds, growing up in a conservative Christian home with Monsanto-friendly church friends and hippie-dippy free-love compost-building farming friends, I decided to reach out and wrestle with this taboo subject. At least, it's taboo in most churches. Goodness, if you dare to question the styrofoam plates at the next potluck, the elders brand you as a commie pinko cosmic-worshipping liberal.

What my friends in the Christian community do not understand is that to the environmentalist, stopping by for a Happy Meal on your way to a Right-to-Life rally is as hypocritical as save-the-tree but kill the unborn baby. The result of all this is that the faith community views the environmentalists as creation worshippers and the environmentalists view the faith community as creation destroyers.

May I offer a bridge? I call it creation stewardship as an expression of Creator worship. Does God care if we humans take care of His stuff? Is it His stuff? Does God care if we honor the pigness of pigs, or are pigs just mechanical expressions of particulate matter upon which humans may innovatively manipulate to their hearts' content? While surely mechanical things do occur in life, I would argue that life, that biology, is far more than simple mechanics.

Perhaps one of the single largest distinguishing factors is that living things can heal. If a wheel bearing thumps, you can apologize to it, rest it, lubricate it, but it will continue to thump. But living things that thump can put on new skin, new bark, respond to compost or bone broth. Living things can heal.

My dad used to admonish us: "Remember, machines don't forgive." What he meant was that if I mishandle a chainsaw and it cuts off my leg, the chainsaw feels no remorse. It's just an inert chainsaw and couldn't care less that it just amputated my leg. Living things, and people, of course, can forgive. A mistreated plant can be nursed back to health with apologetic care. A wounded emotion can be made right with proper apologies and attention.

All of life is pulsing with sentience. From the sunflower that follows the golden orb across the sky to the bacterial nutrient cafe in the soil trading plant sugars for dissolved minerals, life's choreography is both awesome and mysterious. The more we know the more we know we don't know. The industrial/mechanical mindset wades into this mystery like a bunch of swashbuckling Conquistadors, patenting, manipulating, deleting, adding.

Why does an earthworm turn right? Why does the urea in cow urine have one more electron than manufactured urea? Why do pigs look the way they do and chickens look the way they do? Are pig tails there to be cut off in order to keep the pigs from cannibalizing in factory houses? Are chicken beaks there to cut off so they don't eat each other in factory houses?

Does anyone want to live in a world where life is nothing more than re-arranged parts? The reason this is important is because ultimately our treatment of each other as humans extends philosophically and spiritually from our treatment of all life. If life is no more sacred than a car or plumbing fitting, the respect for other viewpoints, cultural differences, vocational choices, is unnecessary.

A farm that honors the pigness of the pig, the essence of pig, is one that illustrates an ethical framework for honoring the Tomness of Tom and and Maryness of Mary. How we respect and honor the least of these creates a worldview about how we honor the greatest of these—each other.

When the industry searches for the stress gene on a pig in order to eliminate it from porcine DNA, it dishonors the very sentience of the pig to know when and what irritates its well-being. That anyone thinks it noble to eliminate the stress gene should make us shudder. Factory farmed pigs are stressed, horribly stressed. But the answer is not to eliminate the stress gene so that we can freely assault their pigness more egregiously without sentient repercussions.

The answer is to contrive a production model that honors the pig's essence, that captures the pig's natural inquisitiveness, digging capabilities, and olfactory gifts. At our farm, we don't put rings in the pigs' noses to keep them from digging. Instead, we use electric fence to control where they dig—kind of like a safe and directed place to play. A pig playpen, if you will. Children in playpens can be happy for hours; pigs in places where they can explore and do important disturbance functions fully express their pigness.

At our farm, we don't use roll away nest boxes for laying hens. While this may sound silly to some, I've spent many an hour watching hens on nests. They don't sit there placidly. Even in commercial flocks of a thousand birds, when a hen enters a nest to lay, she's all business and all about building a nest. She takes a piece of bedding from one side and places it on the other. She moves things around with her wings even, fluffing, settling, positioning.

To deny her all those nuances of nesting somehow seems demeaning, disrespectful. Can you taste it in the egg? No. Could any laboratory measure the qualitative difference between an egg laid in a hay nest compared to one laid in a roll away box? No. But it seems to me that the hen has a more pleasant experience when she can nestle down in a nest.

And somehow I think that level of care translates itself into caring for people, caring for spouses (not that they aren't people too—ha!), caring for our community. Plenty of studies show a propensity toward uncaring-ness moves people toward abusive relationships. This is why I'm such a big believer in children's gardens and caring for animals. Living things respond to care.

When I transplant tomatoes, I don't just go through the motions. I'm speaking, either audibly or in my mind, to each plant, beaming encouragement: "Okay, little guy, get going. Here you go, little root hairs. Here's a nice lump of compost--enjoy your first breakfast outside." When doing this with my grandchildren, they consider such talk completely normal. Only adults think talking to tomato plants is weird.

Is it too far out to suggest that coarseness toward life translates to coarseness in political discourse? That if we view our ultimate place as manipulative over life, we'll view our ultimate cultural fulfillment as manipulative over other cultures? Why is it so hard for us to connect these dots?

If my faith community would embrace this creation stewardship, life essence idea as an act of worship toward God who owns it all, we could be viewed as nurturers rather than rapists. We would be viewed as the ultimate caretakers rather than the ultimate conquistadors, who by the way, invoked God in all their trepidations. To invoke God's blessings on a Concentrated Animal Feeding Operation (CAFO) or red dye 29 is identical both in worldview and action to the conquistadors invoking God's blessings to destroy the Incas.

A farm that truly demonstrates life's sacredness, that in Biblical parlance is "fearfully and wonderfully made," is a place where life expresses its physiological distinctiveness. That looks a lot more like pigs in the woods, pigs in pasture, pigs on compost, than pigs in tiny cells with cut-off tails, living on concrete slats suspended above slurry excrement; no sun, no grass, no butterflies. Failing to consider the dullness of life for the pigs leads directly to failing to consider the dullness of life for people. We become what we create.

Life is more than mechanics; it's vibrant, sentient, alive. In all our techno-sophistication, we have not captured life. Life captures us, dependents in this great choreography of creation. Filling our place humbly, respectfully, opens the way for us to understand our stewardship boundaries and responsibilities. Ultimately, honoring life is a catalyst for honoring God.

14

Stewarding Words

written in 2016

The *Mother Earth News* tribe has a long, illustrious and storied reputation as stewards of the earth. As a young teen I grew up with the magazine's launch during Viet Nam, Woodstock and Watergate. Through it all, our tribe, politically bi-partisan from liberal to conservative, religiously diverse from Christians to Gaia worshippers, agrees on at least one thing: earth stewardship.

We all feel a sense of deep responsibility toward breathable air, healthy soil, and potable, plentiful water. We all feel personally assaulted when public and private interests desecrate, pillage, and attack these precious resources upon which we all depend.

As if that were not a big enough burden for this caring, thinking, participating tribe, we now have a new stewardship responsibility. As a wordsmith, performer, and idea marketer, I think one of our biggest new challenges is safeguarding our vocabulary. Our tribe developed a vocabulary to promote and explain our thinking. We popularized these words. But today, powerful interests threaten to change their meaning; our communication pathways depend on preserving these words.

Here are some that awaken my ire. Genetically modified organism (GMO) is losing ground in the court of public opinion, so the scientific community is floating a rename: genome editing. This is certainly clever, but we as a tribe must keep using GMO, especially since we're gaining ground.

The word edit certainly sounds more benign than the word modification. One conjures up helpfulness; the other tyranny or domination. Had the GMO lovers used the phrase genome editing at the outset, I daresay our side would have had far more difficulty arousing the public from its lethargy. Words are powerful and the industrial food/farm community hunkers down in focus groups with some of the brightest, sharpest communicators in the world to create a new vocabulary. The new words, of course, all tend to paint the opposition in a poor light while painting the miscreants in a positive light.

Monsanto says it's the true repository of sustainability— sustaining human life by growing more food. Regardless of how the current industrial orthodoxy promotes genome editing, we need to keep using GMO, or perhaps we should come up with something better, like DNA execution. Why not fight fire with fire?

Ready for another one? The phrase free range, used by poultry producers seemingly forever, conjures up a certain mental image: chickens out on green grass, not crowded tightly, scratching, pecking and expressing their chicken-ness. The phrase creates bucolic pastoral backdrops in the mind's eye.

But the official government definition is simply freedom to extend all appendages to their full limits. Now I beg you, would any reasonable person come up with that meaning for the phrase free range? Of course not. It's a complete adulteration of the phrase. It means that as long as a cage is big enough to allow full extension of wings, legs, or heads, that's free range. This definition has nothing whatsoever to do with being outside, sunshine, exercise, grass, bugs, scratching, pecking or fresh air.

This is one reason I prefer the phrase pastured poultry. The problem with government definitions is that they obfuscate more often than providing clarity. Who but a government agent would think that free range poultry has nothing to do with the outdoors? People who love genetic modification will also love vocabulary modification.

Grass fed beef is, rightfully, a new darling in the ecological and integrity food movement. But we're seeing all sorts of grain fed outfits using the term grass fed and creating many confused consumers as a result. Their justification is that if the animal eats any grass at all, then it's grass fed.

When foodies and alternative farmers developed the term a couple of decades ago, it was meant to differentiate herbivores that ate an exclusive grass-based diet from those who ate any grain. This exclusivity carved a market niche and point of discussion for thousands of conversations. Now, the term is practically meaningless as a point of differentiation.

I developed the term salad bar beef in order to re-stimulate conversations and therefore the important role of farmers in educating folks about why we do what we do. And how it's different than how others do what they do. The industry hates differentiation.

Notice any food recall, and you'll see a dozen brand names coming out of the same processing plant. It's all the same stuff, just different brand names. As the food industry continues to centralize and the big guys buy not-so-big guys, this product and brand name homogeneity escalates. Finding and using a vocabulary of specificity will become more and more important for our tribe. In order to speak comparison and clarity into the food and farm system, we'll need to know our terms, own our terms, define our terms, and defend our terms.

This is no bigger or smaller a stewardship commitment than compost vs. chemical fertilizer and mulch vs. herbicides. Those discussions define our tribe and our movement; we can be thankful that clever people gave us an ecological vocabulary. Think about the gift that Elaine Ingham's soil food web phrase brought to our movement a few years ago. Such a pregnant phrase stops simplistic chemical-pushers in their tracks and demands respect. That is all part of our stewardship.

Look what has happened to the word organic since J.I. Rodale first invented the term in the late 1940s. We all knew what it meant, but once the industry and the government owned it, all sorts of questionable nuances are now done in the name of organic. In poultry, for example, organic requires access to pasture or outdoors (notice the conditional) but with a huge caveat: inclement weather or health of the bird. If either of those is an issue, then outdoor access is unnecessary.

Well goodness, health of the bird can be used to justify anything. Now that the National Organic Standards Board has eliminated the mandatory sunset clause for questionable ingredients, the downward compromise in certified organics is inevitable. I for one am disappointed that Wal-Mart is now the largest retailer of organics.

We should be encouraging folks not to go to Wal-Mart. Since when is shipping money to Bentonville, Arkansas suddenly a beacon of light? Every day I meet farmers desperate for a couple more customers so they can leave their town job and be full-time farmers. This dream is not helped by Wal-Mart siphoning off sincere, well-meaning customers from the local food scene. Industrial organics is not what Rodale had in mind, but it has usurped that local-centric multi-speciated self-regenerating ideal.

Cornucopia, a non-profit organic industry watchdog, is a small David against a marketing Goliath, trying to bring sanity and accountability to the organic adulteration juggernaut. Their aerial pictures of factory organic poultry operations show the blatant disregard for the standards by the large certified players. The USDA couldn't care less about this flaunting of the regulations. How many Americans buy those scofflaw eggs at Wal-Mart and think they're really changing the foodscape?

Next door is a true blue integrity farmer producing pastured eggs light years better than those organic eggs—even if they're not fed organic-licensed feed. This is why I like the term beyond organic. Again, it's a conversation starter, rather than promoting hardening of the categories. The organic license is not comprehensive.

The terms humane and animal welfare are being misused. If a third party certifier demands a vegetarian only diet for chickens or pigs, for example, it means those animals cannot be placed on pasture or outdoors. Any outdoor access will enable these omnivores to eat a worm or bug of some kind; hence, not a vegetarian diet.

I submit that denying omnivores the chance to eat an insect or bug hurts humane or animal welfare considerations. Since when did these kindness terms become co-opted to mean something entirely different? It's not kind to a pig to deny its ability to root in the soil and eat worms. It's not kind to a chicken to keep her from ever chasing down a grasshopper. And yet that is exactly what these terms have come to mean.

Finally, the term safe. The industrial food complex wants

folks to believe that the term safe is objective, but it's not. Safe from what? Today's orthodoxy uses the lethal dose idea to determine safety. In other words, if it doesn't kill you right away, then it's okay.

Safe has also come to mean sterile. But food should not be sterile; it should be full of micro-organisms: life. Coca-Cola is safe, but raw milk is unsafe by this standard. And yet I would suggest that drinking a glass of Coke every day is more unsafe than drinking a glass of good raw milk.

Life is fundamentally spontaneous. It's not empirical. Risk is hard to measure. Is manufactured cheese-like substance that won't mold for a year when squeezed out of a tube safer than cheese that grows mold and walks off the table in a couple of days? These are questions of worldviews and the conflict of a million conversations.

As the industrial orthodoxy tries to confuse and adulterate, our side must commit ourselves afresh to defending and stewarding our lexicon. We all owe Douglas Gayeton a debt of gratitude for his Lexicon of Sustainability, trying to tackle key words and hold them in purity for future generations. I hope we'll embrace the stewardship of our language the way we've embraced stewardship of the earth. These two missions are inseparable and equally important. Now go have a meaningful conversation, but know your terms.

15

Homestead Grazing

written in 2017

Too often small acreage people feel left out of the grazing discussion. Listening to commercial farmers and ranchers talking about moving 200 cows around an intricate grazing mosaic may be exciting, but is such discussion practical for someone with one or two acres?

For all you folks with small acreages, rest assured that one of the most beautiful aspects of this choreography is its applicability to all scales. The only thing that is scale prejudicial (against small acreage) is that the cost per acre of infrastructure (fence and water line) is higher.

Stopping and starting a fence is expensive: tie-off insulators, gates, braces. Stopping and starting water lines is expensive: valves, Ts, and pipe clamps. Running a long water or fence between stops is easy and cheap; it's the starts and stops that add a lot of cost. Thus, the cost per acre to put in the incumbent fencing and water for small parcels is more per square yard than large parcels.

Otherwise, the principles are close to identical. Let's start with the basics. Animals are supposed to move. Sanitation, vegetation pruning, and defecation spreading require timely movement. The pluses are enormous and myriad. To be sure, much of the worst land management in the world occurs on small acreages where dirt lots and dirt loafing areas build up pathogens, create erosion-prone bare soil, and waste precious manure and urine.

Animals that move need water, shelter, and control proximate, in real time. The neighbors don't want our animals roaming over their property and our gardens don't want sheep and goats munching down the beet tops. Keeping animals where they are supposed to be while they're supposed to be there is perhaps the first ingredient in the recipe for controlled grazing.

This control mechanism can take many different forms depending on species, size of area, and number of animals. The control—and protection requirements—for poultry is quite different than for cows. This is why small-scale controlled poultry grazing often centers around some sort of portable all-purpose structure. At a liberal 5 square feet per bird, even a 10 ft. X 10 ft. paddock is plenty for 20 laying hens per day. Portable coops are the name of the game.

When just a handful of animals is involved, completely contained portable structures are often better than electric fencing. My grandson's ram does well in a 10 ft. X 10 ft. lightweight wooden corral on rubber tires. Even a 10-year-old can push it around and it doesn't require energizers, ground rods, and separate shelter. We call it the Rambler. It can be used like a biological weed eater around the yard, farm buildings, and homestead without running electric wires everywhere.

Few people could be a bigger fan of electric fence than I, and yet often, with small livestock and poultry, a completely portable housing situation is easier to work with than electric fence. Anyone familiar with our farm knows that we still use and encourage completely portable chicken shelters for meat chicken production. With poultry, it's not just enough to keep the birds controlled; you have to also keep predators out. That changes the game and makes the portable accommodations competitive with electric fence systems.

With cows, whether a couple of beef steers or a milk cow, seldom does a physical portable corral system compete with electric fencing. The reason is that due to their sheer size and strength, large animals can tear up flimsy portable physical structures. The sheer weight required to make them strong enough makes them cumbersome (heavy) to move around.

The basis for all controlled grazing is the animal unit (AU) per day. To know how much to give them for a day, you need to know how much forage is available. Developing this sense is called the grazier's eye. The cow is the grazer; you're the grazier. If you're moving her every day and recording how much area you gave her, quickly you'll get a good sense of how much area she needs for one day.

For example, if I give the cow 200 square yards and she has a lot left over in 24 hours, I'll adjust it down tomorrow. The key is knowing how much area she got in order to make an adjustment. If I decide to adjust it by 10 percent, then I'll give her 180 square yards tomorrow. If 20 percent, she'll get 160 square yards, and so forth. Just eyeballing the area and running fences by guess and by golly won't develop the grazier's eye. This is the technical science part.

While controlled grazing involves math and science, it also involves artistry. You're using the 4-legged mower to prune and freshen up the biomass. I view it as painting the landscape canvas with a portable sauerkraut vat. The electric fence becomes the steering wheel, brake, and accelerator on that pruning instrument, which in this case happens to be an extremely intelligent and lovable animal.

In this column, I don't want to get bogged down in electric fencing types; my purpose here is to promote the movement because it is key to the health of everything. Generally, cows do fine with a single wire; sheep and goats need three; pigs need two when they're small and are fine with one once they're up to 150 pounds. The key to using electric fence is consistency, visibility, and a hot spark.

Controlled or rotational grazing seems like magic when you start doing it. What seems like a daunting amount of work—"what? Move the cow every day?"—actually becomes a enjoyable desire. The reason is that the animals respond to the fresh salad bar every day and the forage salad bar responds positively to the extremely strategic pruning. Since forage grows in an S curve, controlled grazing enables you to time the pruning (grazing) at the top of the S before plants head into senescence. The whole idea is to increase the amount of time the plants enjoy their juvenile growth period, thus capturing more solar energy into biomass.

How does this look in practical terms? Let's assume you have one cow and two acres. Under continuous grazing regimens, that pasture yields (in our part of Virginia) 80 cow-days per acre, or 160 for the two acres. Since a year is 365 days, that's only enough for half a year. Generally, a farmsteader will buy hay to feed the cow for the other half of the year.

But let's assume that we use electric fence and give the cow access to only as much pasture as she needs for a day. If the forage is 50 cow-day in volume, she needs 1/50th of an acre, or about 100 square yards. Ideally, that would be offered at 10 yards X 10 yards—animals graze squares more efficiently than rectangles. Tomorrow, she moves to the next spot; the next day, to the next spot.

Under this regimen, it will take 100 days to cover the whole 2 acres. That means the first paddock grazed will have had 99 days to recover. In areas with rainfall above 20 inches per year, a 3-month rest period during the growing season is usually adequate for the forage to regrow to pre-grazing volume. The second grazing cycle takes another 100 days. Now we've grazed 200 days and have a third cycle to go. Suddenly, we don't need to buy any hay.

On our farm, using this practice, we've moved the production from our county average of 80 cow-days per acre to an average of 400. On leased pasture, we've consistently achieved a doubling of production in one year by moving from continuous to daily-move rotational grazing.

Many people ask why the daily move is so important. How about once a week, or every few days? Having worked with this for a lifetime, I can assure you that the daily move is magic. First, it keeps the animal on the highest consistent nutritional plane. Second, it maximizes manure and urine application. Third, it creates the most disturbance for the shortest period of time, which is good for the ecology of the plant and the soil. Fourth, the animal enjoys a routine and builds not only knowledge but trust in the system and in you, the grazier.

As for water, I'm a huge fan of pipe. Carrying water is time consuming and arduous. Run a hose and enjoy on-demand water. It's not that expensive.

Finally, shade for your cow in these little paddocks can be provided with nursery shade cloth atop a simple tinker toy-type lightweight portable structure. Just 20 square feet is more than enough for one cow. That's 4 ft. X 5 ft. and only 5 ft. high. That can easily be built light enough to push around by hand, kind of a glorified wheel barrow.

Daily moves increase your learning curve speed. If you're moving once a week, you'll only learn at 50 pings per year. But if you move daily, you can actually learn at 356 pings per year. This is all theory, of course. In actual practice, you'll be gone once in awhile and give a big enough paddock to last for a few days. You'll have more fertile areas and less fertile areas so the paddocks will adjust in size to accommodate the thickness and richness of the sward in that particular spot. But the more often you move the animal, the quicker you will master the technique.

The choreography of this intricate human-animal-ecology dance offers a lifetime of discovery nuances. Today is the best time to start.

16

Composting Manure

written in 2017

Anyone raising livestock on a farmstead knows that much of animal husbandry revolves around properly handling manure. To be sure, one of the greatest benefits of livestock is their manure. It's certainly as valuable as whatever milk, meat, or eggs the animals produce. Unfortunately, however, this asset is rarely leveraged to its full potential. Maximizing that value through composting is what I want to address in this topic.

Although our family always had a compost pile—kind of a glorified weed pile—next to the garden, my real epiphany on manure management occurred as a teen. Our farm was a gullied, rock pile of poverty when my mom and dad purchased it in 1961. Dad developed a portable electric fencing system and began rudimentary cattle rotation. He hauled in corn cobs from the local grain elevator (this was before combines) and spread them on the rocks.

We put up loose hay with an old-fashioned hay loader, using a grapple fork to unload it in the barn. Dad developed a V-slotted feeder gate that spanned the hay storage area so the cows could feed off the face of the hay. As they ate, we simply moved the long gate a few inches forward. This was certainly an easy way to feed hay, but it created a problem: manure and urine buildup.

The concrete floor soon became covered several inches deep with manure. We'd pitchfork out the chaff and leavings that would collect in front of the hay gate, but it did little to absorb all the sloppy droppings. Throughout the winter, then, we would clean out the floor and spread it on the fields with the manure spreader. What we noticed was that the material we spread in January did practically nothing to help fertility, but what we spread toward the end of the winter and in early spring—right as the grass greened up—gave dramatic results.

Same material; same field; different time. Then came the epiphany: the dead-of-winter material could not be metabolized by the dormant soil micro-organisms and it simply leached out or vaporized away by springtime. Capitalizing on the manure asset required more strategic thinking about application timing, which inevitably necessitated storage.

Putting it outside would expose it to the same elements that robbed us in the first place. It was too sloppy to compost, and besides, compost needs about 50 degrees Farhrenheit in ambient temperature in order to get started. The ideal, we believed, was in situ storage, protected from the elements, and then composted. That meant we had to get our carbon higher in the animals' lounge area.

Good composting requires balancing five things: carbon (C), nitrogen (N), moisture, air, and microbes. I've never had a problem getting enough microbes; if that's an issue, you can add some soil. Animal manures contain lots of microbes.

Manure is high in nitrogen; too high to compost. Different animals generate different C:N ratios in their raw excrement. Cows are about 18:1; chickens 7:1 (this is why we refer to poultry manure as hot). By the same token, carbon sources vary in ratio. Sawdust is about 500:1; wood chips (no leaves) 250:1; deciduous leaves 35:1; straw 100:1. Ideally, compost should be about 25-30:1.

Again ideally, on the farm the proper balance and mixing occurs by default. As much as a pasture-based farmer like me would love to see animals outside all the time, that is neither desirable nor practical during some times of the year. Chickens do not enjoy a couple feet of snow. In a cold snap, water lines freeze and the basic requirements of animal care become arduous.

In the late winter, during thaw, a cow herd can do significant damage to the soil through pugging. Ditto pigs. Solving our conundrum of in situ storage and proper C:N ratios led us back to the ancient practice of bedding, or the static manure pack. Gene Logsdon probably described this as eloquently as anyone in his little book *Holy Shit: Managing Manure to Save Mankind*. Don't let the title dissuade you; it's a great little tome.

I call the bedding pack a carbonaceous diaper. The deeper it is, the better it works. It's a magnificent sponge that performs many functions. First, it absorbs fragile nutrients, chemically bonding them to carbon at the molecular level to stabilize everything. The static pack holds both vaporization (smells) and leaching (groundwater contamination) in check. Stopping vaporization is especially enjoyable because one of the most common nuisances around housed or sheltered livestock is noxious odors, which represents fertility and capital escaping from the farm.

Old-timers in our neighborhood tell me that one of the

first chores for farm boys was picking up cow pies in the barnyard, putting them in a wheelbarrow, and toting them into the barn. Covered with straw and then stepped on by the animals, these outside fertility pies suddenly enjoyed the protection and stability afforded by being placed inside.

Second, the deep bedding gives animals a warm, soft, comfortable lounging area. Concrete is as harmful to animals as it is to humans. Mud is even worse. Offering a clean lounge area bears health dividends to the flock or herd. Although the bedding pack is not warm to the touch, it never freezes. The anaerobic fermentation process creates enough heat that it stays well above freezing even when the ground is frozen.

Third, deep bedding offers a medium for nematodes and other pathogen-fighting microbes to proliferate. This may be one of the biggest benefits because it speaks to the heart of the livestock housing problem: sickness. While bugs tend to have a negative inference in our culture, the truth is that most bugs (layman's term for microscopic bacteria, fungi, and creepy crawlies) are good. The trick is to provide a habitat that allows the good guys to beat the bad guys. You can call this an immunological terrain if you want.

In order for such a terrain to exist, it must have mass, depth, thickness. It can't exist in thin landscapes any more than a softball-sized compost pile can exist. Herein lies the bugaboo. Livestock housing facilities need to be designed so that bedding depth can be significant (12-48 inches) without compromising structural integrity. Sill plates, walls, feeding boxes—everything needs to able to accommodate this bedding buildup. Not one in a hundred barns or farm buildings are designed to handle deep bedding, arguably the single biggest travesty in rural America.

On our farm, we use different procedures for different animals. Herbivores eat hay out of hanging boxes that we can crank up with a hand winch (like curtains) as the bedding builds. We add corn to the bedding. When the cows come out to graze in the spring, we put in pigs, who seek the fermented corn and aerate the pile, converting it to aerobic compost. When the pigs finish, we spread it on the fields.

Chickens don't pack the bedding down like herbivores because they can scratch. Also unlike cows, the chickens are not as easy to chase outside while adding mid-winter carbon. Before the layers come into their solar heated plastic covered tall tunnels for winter, we put in 12-18 inches of wood chips. That's enough carbon to handle all their manure for the 100 days they'll be inside, at a density of one bird per three square feet. We spread whole grains (wheat, barley, rye, oats) on the bedding each day to stimulate scratching. Some of the grain sifts down into the bedding and sprouts, further encouraging the birds to scratch and seek out those tasty morsels. All this scratching and aeration yields a wonderful compost to spread on fields in the spring.

Pigs are a little different. Unlike herbivores and chickens, they pick a toilet area. This means they root around the rest of the space, but leave their toilet area undisturbed. We give them junky hay or corn fodder each day; they eat half and strew the other half over their toilet area and churn it into their unsoiled bedding. In the spring, we simply mix the toilet area with the non-toilet material, let it sit for about three weeks, then spread it on the fields. The toilet area provides enough moisture, nitrogen, and microbes; the non-toilet area provides the air and carbon.

During the bedding-building period, minerals, wood ashes or any other soil amendment desired can be added. The biological and enzymatic activity during the process enhances the whole, creating more fertility punch. Compost is magic. Seeing composting not as a separate process from everything else, but actually designing composting into the housing/sheltering system takes much of the work out of the process and yields symbiotic returns.

Deep bedding creates efficiency because instead of routine clean-out, it requires only annual clean-out. That moves the clean-out from a chore to a shindig, which is cool. Throw a party; invite your friends—tell them to bring pitchforks and wheelbarrows. It's a time of celebration, of capturing wealth. What's not to love?

This system requires carbon, lots of carbon. If all the money spent on chemical fertilizers were spent instead on carbon, we'd have a fundamentally different culture. Diseased, invasive, and poor-quality trees would be chipped, healing and enhancing our forests. No more fires. Thousands of jobs in the carbon sector would replace thousands of soldiers fighting to insure cheap petroleum. Earthworms would rejoice over receiving compost rather than chemical 10-10-10.

Housing animals sometimes is okay. It's actually beneficial if the design, protocol, and system move toward compost and all its magical attributes.

17

Feeding Chickens

written in 2017

Because they are omnivores, chickens are perhaps the most salvage-savvy critter on the farmstead. Historically, their cleaner-upper role predated compost piles for getting rid of food wastes, garden wastes and generally ridding the farmscape of ticks and beetles.

The chicken's compatriot, of course, was the pig, especially on dairies and cheese making outfits. A pig can scarf down copious amounts of whey and spoiled milk. Chickens like these liquid feedstuffs too, but it takes a lot of chickens to eat 5 gallons of whey. Amazingly, in the days prior to chemical fertilizer and mechanization, when grain was still expensive, skim milk offered a more reliable and cheaper protein feedstock than soybeans. My, how times change.

Pat Foreman, chicken whisperer and guru of urban flockering, says that we have enough kitchen and food scraps in America to feed every egg layer we need to provide all the eggs we use. Can you imagine a country without a single commercial egg outfit, not because the population ate no eggs, but because the food system was so tightly integrated in a closed-loop model that chickens intercepted the waste stream?

Now wouldn't that be a place to live?

Laying hens, like humans, need both protein and carbohydrate. While I'm a huge fan of feeding table scraps to chickens, and have done so all my life, it's often not a totally balanced diet. Because a bird's metabolism is high, it's less forgiving in nutritional shortfalls than other animals. Relative to muscle tissue, the bird packs on less fat than herbivores and pigs.

Probably some of that lower stored energy physiology is just to keep her from being too heavy to fly. After all, a chicken is a bird. Sometimes we have to remind ourselves of that. Birds have high metabolisms. They need to eat frequently and they can't gorge themselves today and sleep it off over the next two.

If you think you're going to feed your chickens on kitchen scraps alone, you need to supply a constant, steady plate. Often, that is not the way kitchen scraps develop. One day you have a bucket full and the next nothing—especially if you eat out for a couple of meals.

Perhaps no one has written more creatively and definitively on this subject than Harvey Ussery in *The Small-Scale Poultry Flock*. I won't go over his creative ideas here; just read the book. But one of the things he does is composting kitchen scraps with worms. That way the worms offer a steady protein source during the ebb and flow of kitchen and garden wastes.

Worms also turn carbohydrates into protein. A chicken needs somewhere around 14-16 percent protein. If you're not familiar with ratios, corn averages around 7 percent protein. Some of the heritage chicken varieties are much higher, even more than 10 percent in some cases.

The main thing to remember when feeding food and

garden wastes, however, is that much of the weight is water. So when you look up how much feed a chicken eats in a day, you'll need to multiply by at least a factor of three to adjust for moist feedstocks.

For dry feedstocks, a healthy, productive dual-purpose laying hen will eat 5-6 ounces a day. This would be a total mixed ration commonly available from a feed supply store. Realize that at a factor of three, this turns into more than a pound a day. If the material is really juicy, like tomatoes or lettuce, the factor should be four or five. Then the problem becomes so much volume the bird cannot ingest enough to satiate her needs because the crop/gizzard/digestive tract simply can't hold that much material. Can you imagine a human trying to stay satisfied on nothing but cabbage and lettuce?

She needs both energy (carbohydrates) and protein, not just minerals and fiber. To complicate the food scrap regimen, from any given meal preparation, a nice mix doesn't always occur. For example, peelings from cucumbers may pile up but there is not a commensurate amount of meat scraps for protein.

Fortunately, protein requirements per day are in the ounce range, so a little goes a long way. Worms, grubs, and any other creepy crawly provide wonderful sources of protein. But anything with meat will too.

Old timers in our community tell me that one of the first chores for farm boys used to be shooting, trapping, or snaring a small animal and giving it to the chickens in the winter time when protein-rich bugs and worms were unavailable. A skunk, squirrel, rabbit, possum or raccoon, with belly slit open, offered a welcome feast for protein-starved chickens.

Done once a week, this fresh meat and viscera protein would carry the home flock until the following week. Today, here at Polyface, we routinely throw in road kill or deer carcasses (after we've harvested most of the meat) left over from hunting into the chicken shelters during the winter. They might take several days to actually peck off the final flecks of meat from a carcass, but they will eventually clean it completely and love the choice.

The difficulty in balancing out food and garden-scrap fed flocks is why I recommend having a ration on offer. Even if the birds receive most of their food from scraps, they can always supplement it from the trough. This way you can be sure the birds are getting everything they need and want.

Fortunately, chickens do not watch TV or read advertisements at the supermarket. They are not swayed by marketing slogans or graphic artists. And even though they don't have the biggest brain in the world, it's plenty big enough to signal to their beak exactly what they need to eat. Chickens, like all animals, have a wonderful innate sense of what they need to stay healthy and they will seek out what is necessary.

Having that safety valve of feed on the sideboard ensures that your birds will not suddenly lack an important nutrient. Remember, their metabolism is faster than a cat or cow.

One of the big challenges when feeding food scraps is hygiene and sanitation. As smart as chickens are, I've never seen anyone train a chicken to eat with chop sticks or silverware. If you put in a dinner plate filled with scraps from your kitchen, I guarantee you that your hens will not surround it civilly and reach over the side to peck out the morsels.

One chicken does not defer to another, with proper etiquette decorum, and cluck: "After you, friend biddy." No, they're all over that plate, scratching, pecking, examining with their cocked-head sideways look. In moments, all the plate contents are spread around the pen/yard, rolling around in the bedding or dirt.

When feeding juicy scraps, be sure they are in a pan with a high enough side that the birds can't scratch it all over the area. Not only does that create an unsightly mess, but it also can facilitate parasite ingestion for the flock. Ideally a feeding system that denies the birds actual scratching access is the best. This is why commercially-manufactured feeders contain spindles on top.

A simple exclusion board on top of the pan, allowing side access but not chicken entry, will help keep everything clean. Just be sure that the pan is narrow enough to allow the birds to reach the middle. Of course, big coarse things like garden weeds are great to add to a quasi-composting area. Let this area build up and the ongoing decomposition will help keep it sanitary by default.

Another option is to place the juicy food scraps on a wire mesh or slatted platform so that whatever gets scratched out does not land on the ground or the bedding. The birds will go ahead and pick up dropped morsels from there and the juice will drain below the permeable platform. If you keep the carbon bedding deep enough under this platform, the moisture will feed a gentle decomposition process and the chickens won't drag wetness around the area.

From time to time, move the platform to a new area and let the birds enjoy the worms and bugs that will inevitably be drawn to the wet area. They'll churn it up, adding oxygen, and that will stimulate more decomposition, bugs, and goodies.

Perhaps the most beautiful thing about feeding meat and meal scraps to chickens is that laying hens offer a biological barrier between the scraps and what you eat. Because they convert it to eggs, you're not actually eating what ate what you wouldn't eat. This is a degree of separation that can give all of us peace of mind that we're not going to catch some pestilence from our feathered friends.

Obviously when the hens age and it's time for the stewpot, this separation is not the case, but nature is seldom perfect. After all, we need to build up our immunities too.

In all, I don't know of a more hard-working companion in ecological function than the home laying hen. She offers personality, diligence, and function beyond anything else, clucking happily as she goes about her work and paying dividends in one of nature's most perfect foods. What's not to love about that?

18

Permaculture

written in 2017

I can still remember my first encounter with the term Permaculture. It was a Plowboy interview with Bill Mollison in *The Mother Earth News Magazine* in the 1970s. I remember well how the ideas resonated with me and I resolved then and there to adopt as many as possible in my future farming systems.

In this article, I'll describe some principles and how we incorporate them here at Polyface. The first is high water. Not just water, but high water. The higher the water on the terrain, the more it can be used as it gravitationally moves downhill. We have built more than a dozen ponds over the years and now have about seven miles of water pipe traversing the farm.

A valve roughly every 100 yards gives plenty of access points. None of these ponds dams up ever-flowing streams; they are in valleys to catch surface run-off during special snow melt or rain events. Even the driest landscapes enjoy a flooding event at least once or twice a year. When water runs across the surface of the ground, it means the commons is full. Keeping that water home protects the neighbors downstream from flooding damage. Using it during dry times adds to base flow and keeps biomass growing.

I admit to being a pond-aholic. I'm addicted to this most powerful and profound landscape building block. Sucking water from aquifers and streams depletes the commons; building ponds to hold surface runoff increases the commons. Furthermore, ponds offer riparian habitats for amphibians, aquatic life, and wildlife. You can see how much water you have in inventory. Gravity water is perhaps the most valuable development anyone can bring to a landscape.

Another permaculture principle is stacking. The first significant stacking model we developed on our farm was the Raken House (Rabbit-Chicken). Rabbits are suspended in roomy pens above the floor and chickens run on the floor. Rabbit urine feeds nutrient-rich moisture into the carbonaceous bedding. Chickens scratching in the bedding add oxygen. The combination creates a wonderful composting bedding, eliminating noxious odors even though lots of animals occupy vertical, cubic space rather than just linear space.

By stacking, the infrastructure (building) is far more financially viable because it has more than one enterprise running through it. In more recent years, we've adapted this Raken House concept to winter tall tunnels. This eliminated frozen waterers and offered the advantage of growing vegetables in that bedding compost when the animals come out in the spring.

We've added another permutation to this idea with young pigs on the floor of the hoop house and mezzanine tables for the chickens. Small pigs do not eat chickens but will knock over fragile waterers, nest boxes, and feeders. We mill lumber on our band saw mill to make tables 4 ft. X 8 ft. on legs about 4 ft. high. By placing these tables tight together, we can configure a mezzanine for the chicken infrastructure up away from the pigs. The chickens occupy both the floor with the pigs and the mezzanine. The pigs stay on the floor. Our pigs aren't flying, yet.

This arrangement greatly increases the floor space of the hoop house. A structure that normally would house only 1,000 chickens can instead house 1,500 without sacrificing square footage per chicken. This substantially increases income per square foot and makes such a structure more financially credible. When the animals come out in the spring, we clean out the deep bedding and plant into the rich soil underneath. By rotating between plants and animals, we can hold pathogens in check because hosts change out about the time pathogens proliferate.

Utilizing gifts and talents of animals to accomplish certain tasks is a favorite permaculture concept and one Polyface implements with reckless abandon. Perhaps the most famous is the Eggmobile, which follows the grazing cattle with hundreds of free range laying hens. Mimicking the way birds follow herbivores in nature, this model accomplishes several tasks with one action—another permaculture favorite.

The chickens scratch through the cow paddies and eat out fly larvae. In doing so, they spread the dung on the ground and even incorporate much of it thinly into the soil surface. By turning a small cow pat into a large fertilizer area, the chickens protect the soil from the bitterness that creates a repugnancy zone around cow dung. Cows don't eat around their own manure; chicken spreading eliminates that zone.

Furthermore, the chickens convert newly exposed grasshoppers and crickets into eggs. An acre of pasture can produce more protein in bugs than it can in meat and milk. By converting all that protein into delicious eggs, this procedure generates another enterprise as a byproduct of pasture sanitation. Perhaps most importantly, the sanitation eliminates parasites and greatly reduces flies on the cattle, offering health and comfort. The time savings in cattle care by not having to run them through a head gate or use grubicides and parasiticides is significant.

Another use of animals to perform important functions is in compost making. At Polyface, when we feed hay, we feed it under an awning in a shed. We add a carbonaceous diaper to absorb the 50 pounds of manure and urine generated daily by each cow. This carbon can be wood chips, saw dust, junk hay, straw, crop residue—anything brown. We add a new layer, lasagna fashion, every couple of days.

The heavy cows tromp out the oxygen and the whole bedding pack ferments anaerobically. As we add bedding, we also add corn. The corn ferments in the pack. The pack stays relatively warm even on the coldest days, offering a non-frozen lounge area for the cows even when the ground is frozen two feet deep. When spring comes and the cows go back out to graze grass, we turn pigs into the static bedding pack.

The pigs seek the fermented corn and in doing so aerate, or oxygenate, the bedding pack. Gradually the entire bedding pack shifts over from anaerobic to aerobic compost. Rather than employing expensive and time-consuming sophisticated compost turning equipment, we use the pigs to do all that turning and churning. In essence, we buy equipment for $100 and sell it for $1,000. That's my idea of reverse depreciation. Appreciating equipment is a good idea.

This procedure fundamentally changes the economics of composting because with animals doing the work, we don't have to do it at a scale to re-capitalize the infrastructure that rots, rusts, and depreciates. The profit potential is size neutral. This is just as applicable with two pigs and a couple of cows as it is with 1,000 cows and hundreds of pigs.

Obviously such a system requires buildings that can handle deep bedding. Every time I begin digging into permaculture, I'm struck by how much all the principles depend on design. On our farm, this is dynamically apparent in building design that facilitates deep bedding. A carbon-centric fertility program depends on a deep bedding system under livestock. The deep bedding essentially puts the animals on a compost pile.

Few things are as unhygienic and pathogenic in animal systems as solid concrete floors, slatted floors, or lightly-bedded floors. Microbes need depth (mass) in order to proliferate— just like in a compost pile. Most barn structures, including horse stalls, are not designed to accommodate 3 feet or more of bedding. At a foot deep, the bedding hits sill plates and rots them out. Not a good thing.

Buildings therefore must be designed to handle deep bedding. That enables all the advantages of active composting, manure storage, and eventual pigaerating. A student of permaculture understands quickly that design is the catalyst for synergy and symbiosis. Bad design inhibits functionality.

At the risk of irritating my permaculture friends, I must disclose why here at Polyface we don't jump on the agro-forestry bandwagon, in which trees and shrubs are planted throughout pastures. While this offers a pretty picture from a drone, it's a nightmare for grassland management. Trees interspersed in a pasture are obstacles to hay making and fencing. They make hay dry inconsistently, a real problem for high quality hay making.

At Polyface, we prefer portable shade mobiles to pasture trees. Used like portable trees, shademobiles allow us to concentrate animal lounge areas exactly where the dung will do the most good. Furthermore, portable shade enables us to change the lounge area every time the animals are in the field. It is possible to diversify all the way to inefficiency.

We incorporate the forest into the open land by investing in timber management, which includes chipping diseased, crooked, less productive trees. We fence out the woodlands to protect them.

In this same vein, I'm concerned about a religious adherence to contour lanes for access. I understand using roads as rain gutters, but if every trip across the farm takes an additional 5 minutes due to running hither and yon on the contour, we can soon eat up lots of time and fuel getting from point A to point B. Rigid contour design can be as inappropriate as rigid square, or block design. A happy medium usually captures enough of the best of both worlds.

The whole permaculture notion of designing for maximum energy output for minimal energy input is a goal worth pursuing, regardless of how big or small our farmsteads may be. Utilizing these basic principles can yield economic and emotional benefits, making our operations more profitable and more enjoyable.

Children and Chores

written in 2017

"**M**y kids dawdle. They don't want to do the necessary work around the farmstead that needs to be done. How do I get them on board?" You can see the yearning in the eyes of parents, hoping that their children will embrace a work ethic, a love of self-reliance and sustainability before "Yuck" and the Kardashians jaundice their worldview.

For adults whose literal recreation and entertainment is milking the cow and weeding carrots—we actually find it therapeutic—often our offsprings' reluctance to join in with similar gusto causes frustration, tension, and even battles. If I could offer a guarantee of success in this regard, I'd probably be a full-time family wellness coach doing seminars around the country. I'm no expert, but I do benefit from a farm where four generations currently live, work, love, and fight. Please indulge me some advice on this subject, based on my experience.

From my own childhood, three things that drew me into a love of chores and hard work stand out vividly. First, my parents allowed and encouraged me to develop my own chicken business when I was 10 years old. When I say "my own business" I mean I was the sole proprietor. If friends visited the farm and asked about chickens, Dad and Mom deferred to me.

I can't remember either of them ever explaining the chicken operation to anyone. They would come and find me, putting me on the stage to explain the business. Day-to-day operations? It was sink or swim on your own, buddy. Certainly they were there to console when a predator wreaked havoc. But they did not pick up pieces if I overslept or failed to take care of things. No indeed. I had to hustle to meet schedules. I had to fit my life around chores.

The personal ownership taught me responsibility. If I neglected something and lost a day's production, that suddenly cost me in my pocket. I never got an allowance; all my spending money came from the chickens. I learned how precious and difficult profitability is. Dad and Mom were shepherds for me, but I had to rustle my own feed. I think too often we parents don't realize how much our children can do, and how early they can do it.

I'm a firm believer that part of self-reliance teaching is in childhood, when the ideal time to start a business is somewhere between 8 and 10 years old. If you wait too long, other interests will crowd out the entrepreneurial window of opportunity. It'll become not cool, not hip. Youth leadership organizations like 4-H and church youth groups see a catastrophic fall-off in the early teens as childhood innocence and curiosity give way to sophisticated fashion and the arcade.

Because my chickens were my business, I had to care for them, market the eggs, order feed, clean their quarters. If I didn't do it, it didn't get done, and nobody nagged me about doing it. "But I have to remind my child every day to go do their chores," laments a parent. Okay, get away from it. Turn it over to them as a business. If they don't want it as a business, let it die. Or pay them a caretaker's fee. Few things fire up a youngster more than some money jingling around. Clearly identify the responsibilities and compensation—let them help decide what is fair so they have ownership—and then get out of the way. They'll either thrive or shrivel; if personal ownership and/or compensation won't motivate, nagging won't either.

The second thing that stands out vividly in my memory is that as a child I knew very well that the farm captured my Dad's complete attention and imagination. The farm was never a chore; he never complained about getting up early or staying up late with a sick calf or in order to milk the cow so we could go somewhere. In addition, the farm consumed our recreation time and our sacred calling. We took picnics to the woods, stopped the tractor to enjoy sunsets. We celebrated the farm.

Do you know how many people spend big money to have a farm experience? Agri-tourism now fully supports or supplements thousands of farms. Urban dwellers desperate for a visceral touch of farm life drop thousands of dollars to spend a couple of days doing what we farmsteaders get to do for free every day. Gather eggs. Milk a cow. Plant carrots. Can applesauce. To us it's chores; to them it's the coolest thing since sliced bread.

My parents' interest in everything farming, from production to processing to the latest recipe from Adelle Davis' *Eat Right to Keep Fit* made each day a theater of drama and discovery. Child development books will tell you that more is caught than taught, and for me that was certainly the case. My Dad's zest for innovation, for ecological discovery, was contagious. Mom's homemade everything; the canned goods in the basement—these consumed our lives. We didn't do ballet, little league, or take-out. Not that I'm opposed to any of that, but if you want to live in the country, then enjoy the country. Don't live in the country acting like you live in the city. You can't do it all, so don't even try.

I see country families ripping up the road every day heading to this activity and that activity. Listen, a farm provides enough entertainment and awesome discovery to satisfy any child's spirit. Crawdads in the creek. Building dams in the creek. Fishing in the pond. Taking a nap with a lamb. Eating a juicy tomato straight off the vine. Unless a child is completely messed up, these activities and surroundings are plenty. Generally, if Mom and Dad are enthusiastic about something, the kids will be enthusiastic about it too.

Thirdly, Dad indulged my fledgling and clumsy construction projects. To put this in perspective, you have to understand that my Dad was a journeyman pattern maker in an auto manufacturing company between high school and WWII. He made his own chisels. His hand-made wooden tool box, with calipers, gouges, and scribes is practically a shrine in our farm shop. We don't touch it—it's too sacred. He could make anything and was a true master craftsman.

Me? I'm nothing. Oh, I've built plenty of stuff, but it's not pretty. My middle name F initial stands for Functionality. But growing up, I never, ever remember Dad making a derogatory comment about my 87 degree angles, my crooked gates, my slapped-together projects. He oohed and aahed, encouraged and complimented. Not until I was older did I realize how difficult that must have been.

My dad made furniture, for crying out loud. I've always told my bride of 37 years, Teresa, that I'd love to build her a house one day, but then I quip: "But you wouldn't want to live in it." It would be like the crooked little man in the crooked little house nursery rhyme. Dad's ability to praise in the face of substandard craftsmanship enabled and empowered me to pursue things I never would have if he constantly complained about my bent-over nails and shoddy workmanship. Don't klll the spirit of your child with a "not good enough" prejudice. Of course it's not perfect; and neither was your first project. Fussy parents are child spirit killers. Dads, if you don't know if you're fussy, ask your wife: AND THEN LISTEN TO HER.

This upbringing planted a love for the farm and an insatiable quest for innovation in my soul for which I'll forever be grateful. As our own children came along, Daniel started his rabbit business (now going strong after 28 years) at 8 years old. Rachel started her baking and craft businesses when she was about 6 (girls are always ahead of boys, right?). Both of them hit 20 years old with $20,000 in their bank accounts—none of it was allowance.

Our grandchildren now all have their businesses. Travis is 13 but started his duck egg business at 10. Andrew is 11 but started his sheep business when he was 9. Lauryn, 9, started her exotic chicken business when she was 8 (girls are still ahead). If someone wants to see their animals, I don't show them off; I find the appropriate grandchild to occupy that stage (and I beam from back stage). And guess what? They treat Grandma and Grandpa to ice cream at the baseball game; how about that?

One final idea: never give time oriented tasks; give task oriented tasks. If you say "Pick beans for 30 minutes," where's the incentive to hustle? If you say "practice the piano for 30 minutes," where's the incentive to achieve? All tasks should be clearly defined with a start and stop without regard to time. Appropriate incentives (money, time, treats, etc.) can be offered as a reward for completion.

That way we incentivize efficiency and completion, not just putting in time. When we just require time, we teach dawdling and poor work habits. Oh, and the reward for efficient completion should NOT be another chore. Work should never, ever, ever be given as punishment. Work should be a game. Run competitions: "Who can pick this row the fastest?" Children love competition. Don't let them win every time, either. Children love meaningful reality. They don't like fake work and they don't like shams. They can sense this condescension faster than you can say "Gather eggs."

Farm is theater, vocation, and discovery. Brainstorm how you can lift your language away from complaints and groans to a more can-do, enthusiastic attitude. Restructure your chore ownership and incentives to create personal fiefdoms of responsibility and reward. I don't guarantee it, but the opposite doesn't work a lick. As someone blessed to live with four generations occupying the same place, harmony of purpose and ministry beats every how-to project out there. In the end, it doesn't matter if you have a pretty garden or a healthy cow if the home is a place of tension and frustration. I hope these ideas will encourage you to work hard at creating a team spirit habitat for your kids as the foundation for a healthy, self-reliant, sustainable farmstead.

20

Preserving Food

written in 2017

I've amassed quite a few interesting statistics about food trends in the U.S. over my years of reading. Some that stick out are that a quarter of all food consumption occurs in automobiles. And that's with people having to steer them. Imagine how this will increase when you don't have to hold the sandwich with one hand and turn the steering wheel with the other because of self-driving automobiles.

Another one: the average American spends 15 minutes a day in the kitchen. Processed food, anyone? Right now the hottest food trend is integrity convenience. Around our farm we laughingly say "everyone wants Polyface Hot Pockets." And here's one: 80 percent of Americans, at 4 p.m., have no idea what they're going to eat for supper. Can you bear another? Some 75 percent of all menu decisions are made by people under 10 years old (children).

Even if these statistics are off by a few percentage points, their cumulative import speaks to a profound lack of culinary planning in modern America. On our farm and in our family, we're certainly the exception to the norm. We spend a lot of time doing what old-timers called "laying by." Spending the abundance season preparing for the scarce season was part of every household until extremely modern times.

Today, anyone who puts this much thought and effort into preserving food for the off-season is in danger of being branded some sort of conspiracy prepper. In fact, doomsday sells: just look at the tools for long-term food preservation available today and barring that, the suppliers who will send you food packages that will last a decade. It's big business.

But here at our Salatin homestead—or compound—we don't buy next century food. We grow it or buy it locally and "lay it by." The first is early fruit like strawberries, which we freeze by the quart—after eating ourselves silly. Then come mulberries and about hay time, blackberries. By August the early apples are ripe and we begin canning applesauce.

With a food mill or other squeezing device, we separate the pulp from the seeds and peels after softening them up with heat. This is often a multiple-hands deal, with one person washing them in the kitchen sink and running the stove while others take turns cranking the mill. Canning moves along quickly and at the end of a day, we often have 80 quarts of heavenly applesauce to show for our efforts.

By recording how much we preserve and how much we have left over, we develop a good sense of what we need to get us through until the following harvest. If we eat three quarts of applesauce a week (we work hard and eat heavy) that's 150 for the year. A bushel of apples yields about 15 quarts. Of course, we've dried apples by thinly slicing them and putting them on screens or in a dehydrator.

As the garden comes into its full glory, preservation becomes more serious. Cabbage is one of the first vegetables ready, and lugging our 10-gallon crocks down from the attic is a rite of passage for the season. Shredded and then tamped into the crocks with a weighted lid to keep the mash compressed, sauerkraut offers fermentation benefits and good nutrition.

After the sauerkraut, we clean out the crocks and fill them with cucumbers for my favorite of all: 14 day sweet pickles. In our household growing up, my Mom always made bread and butter pickles and often dill pickles. Not until I began selling at the local curb market (depression-era precursor to today's farmers' markets) did I encounter homemade sweet pickles.

One of the other vendors usually made potato salad to sell, and I would purchase some for breakfast to complement my thermos of raw milk from our hand-milked Guernsey cows. Oh my, she put sweet pickles in that potato salad. I'd never had anything so divine. A couple of years later I met my now-37-year bride, Teresa, in high school and we began dating.

As things progressed, I got invited to the family Christmas gathering. And do you know that there, in a glass tray, I found those same sweet pickles. I determined right then and there I wanted to be a member of this family, and Teresa was the most likely candidate for accomplishing this purpose (she had three brothers, after all). The 14-day pickle is a long process, but Teresa has faithfully continued her family tradition.

One year she found a recipe that purported to do the same thing in eight days. Without my knowledge, she used it thinking she would fool me and save a lot of time and energy. I had no idea, but as soon as I opened that first jar, I knew something was different and wondered aloud. She laughed, confessed, and has never repeated the shortcut. Some things just can't be hurried.

Pickled beets are a favorite at our house, primarily to create the solution for pickled eggs. Few things make as quick and delicious a lunch as a couple of pickled eggs. Beautiful and tasty.

Green beans come next, requiring sitting time with newspaper across the lap to hold the beans and their snapped-off ends. Ideally we do this while listening to a favorite program on the radio or recording (we don't have a TV in our house). I suppose you could watch a movie, but you have to pay attention to what's going on in your lap or you'll have funky things in your green beans. We sure don't want that when the snow is blowing.

Fast on the heels of green beans comes corn, marvelous corn. That's another many-hands-on-deck ritual because it has to be shucked, blanched, and then cut off the cob. Very early in the morning we go through the corn patch plucking the perfect ears. My favorite technique is sitting in the pasture, shucking the corn out in the field with the cows. The friendliest ones come right up and eat the shucks from between my legs, their warm breath and burps adding theatrical dimensions to the process.

We bring the ears into the kitchen, where the table is covered in newspapers to protect it from the wayward juice squirts that inevitably occur during cutting. The blanched ears offer succulent hot kernels for snacking during the cutting process. We spread the kernels on cookie sheets, not quite an inch thick, and lay the sheets in the freezer. By next morning, they're frozen solid but the layers are thin enough to break up. We put the frozen kernels into big plastic bags and during the winter, we scoop the amount we want out of the bag and re-twistie it until the next extraction.

Few vegetables are as versatile as squash. We shred zucchini and can in pint jars that work perfectly for two loaves of zucchini bread. We dice and can summer crookneck squash. Summer produce and herb variety allow us to make relish, which we can in pint jars rather than quarts.

By this time in the season, tomatoes are in full production. The early hesitant ones have been consumed daily but now the vines burst with ripe fruit. We pick them by the bucket full and begin canning. We make juice out of the blemished ones, using the same mill we use for applesauce. The nicer ones we cut up in pieces and squish them into quart jars. Tomatoes are a mainstay during the long winter months, bringing that explosion of taste onto the plate in the darkest and coldest days.

Using a steam juice extractor, we can elderberry juice and lots of grape juice from our vines. We cut it 50/50 with water to drink and it's still plenty strong. At Christmas, our grape juice is the basis for festive punch.

We process chickens almost weekly during the warm season, selling most and keeping the culls—blemished in some way. We cook those in a ginormous roasting pan (as many as we can cram in there), pick the meat off, then dice it up into quart freezer containers for winter casseroles. Of course, we also keep all the broth. The boney carcasses can be cooked down for bone broth.

We also can chicken, or any kind of meat, from pork to beef to venison. The beauty of canned meat is that if the power goes out, it doesn't perish with everything else in the freezer. It's pre-cooked, making quick meals easier. The key to canning meat is to not completely fill the jars. It's tempting to fill jars as full as possible, but if any fat bubbles lodge around the lip of the jar, it won't seal. Leave a good inch of space to insure a good seal.

Of course, many late summer and fall crops do not require any more preservation than putting them in a root cellar or cool basement. Late cabbage, potatoes, carrots, onions, pumpkins, and winter squash will keep until the following spring. A solarium on the house provides fresh lettuce and other greens throughout the winter.

While this is certainly not a comprehensive list, it's a peek into the seasonal food cycle at our house. This is simply how our families do things; it's not a sudden reaction to economic instability or political insecurity. It just flows and fills the larder with homemade. Surrounded by abundant production in season and abundant harvest off season, we're daily reminded of our dependence on and provision from the earth. That's a good way to live.

21

Preparing for Emergencies

written in 2017

S itting in the kitchen/dining room on a sweltering July evening about five years ago, Teresa and I were chatting and reading when suddenly a gust of wind shook the house. Within a minute, debris pummeled the house and the roar of wind sounded like something out of a sci-fy movie.

Almost before we could run around and check things, the back door slammed: in came a terrified apprentice. She had run down from her cottage on the hill, afraid that gyrating trees would crush her living quarters. Moments later, an intern rushed in, seeking solace and shelter.

What we did not know until later was that we were dead center of a weather phenomenon known as a derecho—straight-line winds (as opposed to swirling) up to 100 mph. It had started in Indiana, built up power across West Virginia, and descended on our area in a direct hit. Roofs came off buildings, trees crushed houses and cars, tractor trailers blew off the interstate. It was unlike anything I'd ever experienced.

Within minutes of starting, several interns and apprentices ran to our house, an extremely old and substantial log and brick structure built in 1800. It has stood the test of time. And the dining room/kitchen is below grade about three feet. Within minutes the power went off. We lit a kerosene lantern and as the storm raged over the next 90 minutes enjoyed feasting on ice cream—without knowing how long the power would be off, why not polish off the most delicious and vulnerable item in the freezer?

By midnight the storm was over and we decided to just wait until morning to survey the damage. It was substantial, and the temperature was 100 degrees F—one of the hottest days of the summer. The power was out all over the entire region. The first item was water for livestock; second was shelter. We had herds of cattle on two leased properties, in addition to a herd here at the home farm. We opened a fence and let one herd go to a river to drink. We rushed our generator over to the other herd to run the water pump so they could drink.

At home, with six miles of water line networking from a series of permaculture-style high elevation ponds, gravity kept the water flowing as if nothing had ever happened. All of us had an epiphany that day as we realized the forgiveness, or resiliency, of gravity-based water. In bygone eras, all water systems were gravity based. But cheap and fairly dependable energy made us lazy—and presumptuous.

Developing gravity-based water systems on the farmstead may be one of the single most critical investments to prepare for natural disasters. Water is the foundation of life, and when you have livestock, they don't care if everything thaws in your freezer; they need water, now. Water resources independent of electricity or petroleum are better than money in the bank.

On our farm, we're blessed with enough elevation that we can water all of our pastures from high ponds we began excavating decades ago. If you don't have enough elevation, an option is a turkey nest pond. It's an excavated cistern—just dig a big hole—on top of a hill. You can fill it from lower water sources with a pump but it gives you enough capacity high enough to provide gravity water without any filling for at least several days.

If you're in extremely flat country, you can hoist a cistern up in a tree to gain gravity pressure. Several 250-gallon totes can provide some great security. Obviously, you'll want to hoist them up in the tree BEFORE filling them. Ha! Water pressure is .7 pounds per vertical inch, so even 25 feet offers 17.5 pounds of pressure. That may not sound like a lot, but it sure beats carrying buckets.

Certainly windmills and solar arrays running pumps can reduce dependency on the grid, but nothing is as dependable as gravity. I always joke that when gravity quits, I'm out of here. All American houses are built with water pumps and pressure tanks located in the basement. Imagine if instead all houses had a 1,000 gallon tank mounted right under the roof? A couple of minutes per day of riding a bicycle powering a water pump could fill it and then the attic tank simply feeds the plumbing throughout the day. Real time, on-demand pressure and energy are always much more difficult than periodic bursts coupled with storage.

One of the reasons I like ponds is because I can always see how much water I have. Wells can get contaminated or go dry with nary a warning. Every day I can go to a pond or cistern and measure what I have. It's like looking in a full food pantry. I don't have to run to the grocery store prior to imminent bad weather because our larder is full of canned goods, the freezers are full, and the greenhouse keeps things growing throughout the winter.

Of course, the morning after the derecho, we had more to worry about than water. We had 1,500 chickens walking around dazed. Some 20 portable field shelters were gone. I don't mean scattered around; I mean gone. Disappeared. The blazing sun would put the chickens into stress quickly without shade. We ran the cows to a paddock with tree shading and confiscated their 1,000 square foot shademobile for the chickens.

Drawn to the cool shade, the chickens quickly mobbed into a flock that we surrounded with Premier electrified poultry netting. As we worked through our triage plan, next on the list was a pair of upturned Eggmobiles (portable laying hen houses that follow the cattle herd). These 12X20 ft. structures, hooked together, were on one of the leased farms and had flipped over UPHILL! None of the other dozen Eggmobiles had turned over, fortunately.

The former intern subcontractor in charge of that farm was practically in shock. His first year farming. Responsible for chickens, turkeys, and cattle. Some 800 laying hens wandering around amid the overturned Eggmobiles, wheels and chassis ten feet in the air. We grabbed a generator and a bunch of shop tools, some boards, and chains, and our whole staff (we call it the cavalry) arrived with expertise and tools. Within two hours everything was set upright and the hens happily went to the nest boxes to do their thing.

All five properties where we had livestock had different needs but by the end of the first day, everything was comfortable. A large portion of that efficiency was due to having a community of expertise and infrastructure that could collaborate quickly. Perhaps the best way to prepare for trouble is to create a close-knit and dependable community. Regardless of what happens, it's always easier to go through hardship holding hands with someone.

Now to the infrastructure. Over the next week, while I ran 30 tanks full of gasoline through the chainsaw cutting trees off of fences and getting everything re-secured, the rest of the staff built 20 new chicken shelters. We returned the shademobile to the cows and put the surviving chickens back in shelters.

Compare that to a factory farm with 50,000 chickens and a destroyed house. Those chickens never had a chance. They died. This is not just the resilience that scale can build; it's a testament to the flexibility of portable, lightweight, low-capital infrastructure. Even a devastating loss is not a huge economic hit.

Our electricity came back on within 12 hours. One of our leased farms did not receive power for a week. While I hope to never go through a storm like that again, it did affirm the adaptability of our systems.

Redundancy is the operative word for crisis preparedness. My wife's grandfather always used to say "you can never have too much hay in the barn." This is like saying "your pantry can never be too full" or "the firewood pile can always use another load." Stocking up is part of redundancy. I wear a belt and suspenders—a belt to hold my cell phone and multi-tool; suspenders to hold up my pants.

The hundreds of quarts of summer produce Teresa cans and freezes are not part of a paranoia response; they're just what thinking people do to build redundancy into our provisions. To live day-to-day dependent on the supermarket is as presumptuous and silly as living without financial savings, the proverbial rainy day fund.

Livestock can be resilient too, rather than fragile. A couple of years ago we still had one group of pigs out in the forest glens when a 20-inch blizzard enveloped us. We could not get there for two days, even with the tractor. When we did, the pigs erupted from their leafy nest that they had built, steam rolling off their warm bodies, all healthy and comfortable. Because we select genetics with hardiness at the top of the criteria list, we don't fear every anomaly that comes along.

Simple infrastructure, hardy animals, technical skill, and community support all work together to make crises less strenuous. Travesties will always happen, but we can certainly ameliorate their effect by spending normal times preparing. Now go dig that pond.

22

Spring Prep

written in 2018

Each spring our pastured livestock farm requires a flurry of preparation as we transition from cold to warm. Here in Swoope, Virginia, located smack dab in the middle of the Shenandoah Valley, our frost dates are May 15 and September 15. But plenty of plant growth occurs, both in the garden and in the field, far before and after these official season-changing dates.

Several years ago our farm hosted a pre-vet externship by a local high schooler headed to veterinary school. Living and working on her family's conventional livestock farm provided an epiphany for both of us once she spent a couple of months on our farm, the area's official lunatic farm (at Polyface, we do few conventional things).

Part of her report to the school faculty following the experience included answering the question "What was your biggest takeaway?" The answer shocked me. She said on her family's farm, winter was always seen as a down time, a dead time, in which nothing prepared for spring. Rather, she said farm work simply meant marking time awaiting the change in weather. In contrast, she said on our farm, the entire winter was seen as prologue to the spring. Every project anticipated the seasonal change and leveraged winter's uniqueness to capitalize on spring's opportunities. The point is that our spring starts early in our minds.

In that light, therefore, I begin preparing for spring the previous fall. How we leave the pastures after their final grazing speaks volumes about what they'll look like two weeks after the first warming days of spring. Leaving pastures debilitated and pounded into the ground retards spring green-up by a couple of weeks and reduces the first month's growth exponentially.

As we enter the dormant season, then, we rotate through the pastures in our daily moves highly cognizant of north or south aspect, fertility, and tendency to wetness. At some point, every pasture receives its final graze of the season. Grazing too hard after dormancy means it will have no cover through the winter. Grazing too early can mean that it grows back in those warm waning days of fall and then freezes prior to replacing the energy in the roots expended in sending out those new shoots. This weakens the plant going into winter and simply exacerbates the energy deficiency throughout the winter.

These tensions and delicate intentions in planning the late fall/early winter grazing schedule are all part of the spring green-up robustness—or lack thereof. Generally we try to get through low ground earlier, knowing that at any time heavy winter rain or snow could make them too soft to handle livestock. The north slopes stop growing first; south slopes continue to grow the longest. Beyond those considerations, we also shift our grazing pattern from year to year so that we don't graze off the same paddock at the same seasonal time every year. This management fluctuation encourages sward diversity and ensures that if we weaken one field one year, we will not weaken it the following year. Nothing is perfect; yearly change-up protects the same imperfection from happening on the same field two years in a row.

Once we've finished with stockpiled pasture (often as late as early February) we begin feeding hay in the shed, where we use a deep bedding concept like a carbonaceous diaper. This is the spring fertilizer. The grazing plan minimizes pasture damage during the dormant season; the hay feeding plan leverages this activity to produce the fertilizer (compost) to be applied after spring green-up. By bringing the animals into sheds on deep bedding (up to 4 feet) during the late winter mud season, we protect the pastures from hoof damage.

The dual benefit of protecting pastures and leveraging hay feeding means that we typically begin grazing a month before conventional farmers in our area. When farmers feed hay out on the same fields livestock graze all year, the forage never gets a rest. The constant hammering and energy deficit weaken the plants and they start growing lethargically once the temperature warms.

All of our planning, infrastructure, and composting are geared to reduce hay feeding. In our area, average time on stored feed is 120 days per winter; at our farm we average 40 days, even though we average three times as many pounds of liveweight per acre. This is not prideful; it's paying homage to a system that respects both the limitations and opportunities of nature.

Of course, with the first spring green shoots of forage, we move into what we call the two-week transition frenzy. It starts with fencing maintenance. Obviously we can't move livestock into the fields without good control. During the winter, tree limbs fall, fence posts give up the ghost, startled deer occasionally break a wire. Few things are as enjoyable as making that initial maintenance check list in the spring. It's the coming out day, that first day I can be comfortable in a broad-brimmed hat instead of the knit cap.

Watching the farm wake up is the most profound spiritual and physical rite of spring. But like all of us after waking in the morning, some of the joints are stiff; we need some water; and we need to dress. Fortunately, the ground is damp at this time, enabling us to efficiently pound in fence posts that we've split, sharpened, and stockpiled during the winter.

As important as fencing control is, water is the other critical maintenance issue. On our farm, we have 8 miles of water line bringing gravity-pressure water from high landscape permaculture style ponds around the farm. Although most of it is buried, some pieces are not. With many in-line valves as part of the installation process, we can turn on one leg at a time and check for leaks and malfunctioning valves.

All winter we've watched our many ponds gradually fill with water. By spring, creeks and springs run robustly and all the ponds are full and overflowing. This water abundance meshes perfectly with getting the water system up and running because if we have a major leak, we don't impair our water stockpile by losing some water. A major leak in late summer hurts because these ponds are low and not replenishing. In the spring, water isn't precious like it will be in a couple of months.

Along with fences and water, portable infrastructure must be readied for the season. During the big winter-spring transition, thousands of laying hens must move from their winter protective high tunnels into portable pasture infrastructure. All of those mobile and modular structures need a going-over.

That flapping piece of roof on the front corner; the broken brace in the back. Power washing, cleaning and replacing nest box material. Once the Eggmobiles, Millenium Feathernet, Gobbledygo, Lambrigini, Quacker Box, broiler shelters, and pig shades are occupied, maintenance is much harder. We want to work on them empty.

As each of these items gets finished, we begin that wonderful animal transition from inside to outside. With thousands of critters to shift, we can't get it all done in a day, but it does happen over just a few days. The entire farm undergoes a dramatic shift. The day cows go out to begin grazing again, we retrofit their quarters to accommodate the pigaearators. We try to get pigs into that deep bedding the same day the cattle vacate in order to not lose any time turning that aerobic nutrient pile into beautiful aerobic compost.

As chickens, pigs, and rabbits exit the hoop houses, we set the nest boxes, feeders, and waterers aside and clean out the deep bedding, spreading it on the hungry fields. Ideally, first fed fields are the ones grazed most imperfectly the previous fall. Within a day or two those hoop houses fill up with vegetables and early spring greens. The mountains of composted bedding going onto the fields find ready appetites among the hungry soil bacteria and fungi which express their own frenzy as they awaken to a new season.

Some of this compost, of course, goes to the garden beds. We watch with giddy anticipation for the first shoots of rhubarb and asparagus, knowing that a couple of months later, as spring gives way to summer, the first hay mowing signals the time to quit picking both of those perennial garden plants. The rhythm of the seasons is a beautiful heartbeat on the farmstead; I can't imagine running a factory farm where seasons do not offer sabbaths and sprints.

Winter's transition into spring creates a frenetic conversion as housed animals move outside to pasture, broiler chicks arrive, and electric fences receive much-needed maintenance. Visitors during this seasonal frenzy often can't imagine how we keep it all straight. But two things make it doable; the first is winter planning. During the winter, our whole family and staff spend days planning the calendar, the grazing pattern, where we'll make hay—the whole season. That's all done well before the first green grass shoot signals the frenzy.

Second, many aspects are simply givens. The Eggmobiles follow the cows. The broilers go on high ground. Low fields can only be grazed when they're dry enough. Pigs go into the hay sheds after the cows exit. While to the novice it may seem like a crazy gyration of activity, it's actually a choreography of ballet in the pasture.

23

Loading and Moving Pigs

written in 2017

Every animal has unique management requirements. Volumes seem to be written concerning diet and shelter, but much less regarding the actual logistics of moving them around. Perhaps that's because too often even at backyard scale animals are not moved much. Shame, shame.

Moving animals is the foundation of hygiene and ecological function. Loading animals for movement is critical for harvest. Too often new critter sitters overlook the nuances of animal psychology and then have horrible experiences trying to load their animals.

While one of these columns could no doubt be written for every species of domestic livestock, I'll devote this one to the pig because of all the different animals, the biggest handling nightmares involve pigs. Anyone who has ever raised a pig has what I call a "pig loading" story. I certainly do, dating way back to our first pigs and our profound ignorance.

Perhaps the most memorable was when I was about 15 years old and my older brother was 18. He was a muscular athlete, too. My dad had an appointment at the local locker plant (abattoir) to process our two hogs. We'd raised them on excess milk from our two Guernsey cows, whey left over from cottage cheese production, weeds from the garden and some grain.

Two friendlier pigs could not exist. They were in a typical torn up muddy pig yard near the barn. The oversized lot surrounded by electric fence offered plenty of exercise space. A large wooden box (the shipping container for our 1952 Ford) served as a makeshift shelter. As close to pets as farm animals can get, these pigs enjoyed belly rubs, lots of attention, and plenty of treats. Every time they saw us they would come running, expecting some tasty morsel or manifestation of affection.

The appointed morning of their departure, however, was a different story. We had a low trailer backed up to the electric fence. We got them confined within four gates a bit larger than pallets. With my dad, big athletic brother, and me manhandling the four gates, we expected to ease the pigs over to the trailer and into it. We made a berm so they would not need to step up at all. We figured to scoot the portable corral over and into the trailer. No problem. Piece of cake. These pigs were friends.

Yeah, right. Getting them wrapped in the four-gate square was easy with some fresh Guernsey milk. But as soon as they felt confined, the war commenced (as my grandmother would say). Squealing and pushing from the pigs made the three of us humans feel like we were on a circus ride. Standing on the gates, jostling from side to side, we managed to scoot the pigs about two feet in 15 minutes. My brother and I were supposed to catch the school bus. Dad had to get to his town job.

As time ebbed away, our frustration mounted and certainly transferred to the pigs. Frustration turned to desperation. The pigs, each weighing nearly 300 pounds, literally wore us out. Sweat lathered the three humans; the pigs squealed and lifted the gates with their snouts. The three of us jumped from one gate to the other to counteract the moment's point of attack from our porcine beauties. When we thwarted the pigs' efforts on one gate, they would wheel and attack the opposite gate. We, of course, had to catapult over the contraption to the other side to beat them to the new point of attack.

Before half an hour was up, we could hold on no longer. The pigs lifted up one side before we could get there and with the agility of a hummingbird and strength of an elephant, they escaped to the far side of their paddock and stood there, heads lowered, glowering at us. I think I could hear them say: "You fools. Who do you think you are, trying to outsmart a pig?"

We canceled the abattoir appointment, called it a day, hit the showers, and went on with our day, nursing sores, bruises, and fighting fatigue. After consulting some old-timers in the area, we conceived a new plan. We tucked the electric fence underneath the trailer, made a ramp, and began feeding the pigs in the trailer. It took them half a day to venture up the ramp to their meal. But food is a powerful incentive to a hog, and they could not resist. We fed them morning and evening in the trailer for the next week.

Dad made a new appointment at the abattoir for a week later. By that time, when the pigs saw us coming with a bucket, they would run up in the trailer and wait for goodies. The morning of the departure, Dad simply swung the door closed after they ran in and took the pigs to their appointment with destiny.

Here is the moral of the story and the secret for all pig handling: movement is much easier if the pigs want to go where you want them to go. It sounds ridiculously simple to make such a statement, but every day farmers try to make pigs go where the humans want them go without thinking about how to make such a journey enticing to the pig.

The easiest and quickest way to incentivize a pig is with food treats. And nothing propels a pig forward quicker to a treat than hunger. If you have a move planned, let the pigs run out of feed, or if you feed them daily, skip a day. A 24-hour fast won't hurt the pig any more than it would hurt you or me. But it does wonders to affect the trajectory of the pig. A little planning for the fast can go a long way to making a move efficient.

The next thing to remember about pigs is the extreme lowness of their center of gravity and their sight line. Even a large hog ready to go to the butcher will have a center of gravity no more than 18 inches off the ground. Its eyes will be even lower. When I illustrate this point in my public presentations, I usually get down on the floor, put my eyes about 14 inches off the floor, and crawl around the room describing what I see. If I encounter someone standing, I describe the spindly little leg-stacles and how easily I think I could go through them, kind of like a series of traffic cones.

As humans, our center of gravity is above our belly button—three or four feet off the floor. A 300-pound pig at an 18-inch center of gravity can upend a 200-pound 42-inch center of gravity human before you can say *The Mother Earth News*. I've been made a fool by a pig more times than I care to admit. You can't imagine the leverage and power—and agility—of a pig in a confined situation when it wants to get through you.

To mitigate this physical—and physic—difference, we use swine sort boards. You can make them out of plywood or you can buy them from farm suppliers. I assure you, they are worth their weight in gold. These boards (the purchased ones are generally made of plastic so they're lighter) are roughly 30 inches high and come in various lengths—36, 48, 60 inches. With two handles on the top, they allow a human to create an opaque portable fence. They turn the pig's low sight line into a liability by making the pig think it has come up against an immovable wall.

The fact that the wall moves does not register with the pig. All the pig knows is that it can't see beyond that wall. When it comes to pig handling, these sort boards are probably the best invention ever made. We don't do anything with pigs unless we have several sort boards on hand.

Pigs love to hug the ground. They don't like to walk up chutes or feel a space between them and the ground. Low boy trailers are now so common that most farms do not use elevated chutes to load onto trucks. But if you do use an elevated chute, make sure it's sturdy and has a solid floor. The most functional is a chute with a dirt floor so the pigs never get an elevated sensation. When asking the pigs to jump up into a trailer, a bale of hay or straw to shut off the light between the floor and the ground can help encourage the pigs to climb in. A little feed or some treats sprinkled in the trailer is also helpful. Sprinkling some feed leading up to and then into the trailer gives continuity to the enticement.

Finally, pigs are smart. Building trust with them is harder than any other animal. They size up your intentions and generally don't assume that you have their best interests at heart. Whereas a cow learns quickly to come to an open electric fence gate, a pig does not.

Therefore, we always put a physical gate in the electric

fence. That way when we want to move them to another paddock, the pigs don't have to trust us to remove the electric fence. They are used to scratching and rubbing on the physical gate (we prefer wood because it insulates and therefore can't short out as easily if something goes haywire) so when we open it, they have no reluctance to go through. Once the pigs are 200 pounds or so, they begin to trust and will go through electric fence gates. They never go through as easily as cows, but you can dispense with the physical gate once you've been together several months.

There you have the basics of moving and loading pigs. With these in mind, you can reduce your nightmares and increase your fond memories. In this case, unexciting is a good thing.

24

Critter Services

written in 2018

I n case you haven't noticed, an increasingly vocal minority in our society opposes domestic livestock as morally, if not environmentally, wrong. With sanctimonious fervor these folks decry cows, pigs, and chickens while extolling the virtues, I assume, of bison, prairie dogs, and pigeons.

A turkey is fine if it's in the wild, but if it's in your backyard awaiting Thanksgiving's repast, it suddenly goes from fair to fowl (sorry, I couldn't resist the pun). As scientists delve into the synergistic intricacies of animal relationships in historic ecological templates, we discover more and more the positive work these animals accomplished. From beavers building ponds to bison pruning prairies, the animal contribution protected water and built soil.

As much as some may want to return to those days, I submit that it would be incompatible with modern civilization for a herd of 7 million bison to go marauding through our neighborhood Starbucks. A 15-acre beaver pond across the interstate could be seriously disruptive. Fortunately, domestic livestock have filled these historic roles, working alongside humans to build civilization and give us time to enjoy museums and art shows.

Please enjoy with me, then, a brief look at critter services on the farm. Let's start with birds, otherwise known as chickens. The ultimate sanitizer, the noble chicken stands between the farmstead and pathogens. Our friendly hens eat ticks, grubs, slugs and insects. At our Polyface Farm, the Eggmobiles (portable hen houses) disgorge 800 layers every morning on newly grazed pasture.

The chickens not only eat bugs in the cow patties, and spread them out; they also harvest the tons of newly exposed grasshoppers, crickets and other insects living in the pasture. When the cows prune off the insects' hiding places, the birds harvest them and turn them into fresh eggs. This works around the goat pen or cow milking stand too. Few animals are as energetic and faithful as the chicken for cleaning and disinfecting the farmstead.

Of course, other birds are adept. Guinea fowl not only eat insects; they announce intruders with their distinctive and raucous chortling. Many people believe them to be superior to dogs as security for the homestead. Not to be ignored, ducks provide wonderful bug control in the garden. Unlike a chicken, ducks tend to leave vegetables alone. And an additional plus: they don't scratch up mulch. They're more content to just roam around, waddling from area to area, always in a tight flock, looking for squash beetles, Colorado potato beetles, and other miscreants.

A barnstead with a handful of chickens on patrol has far fewer flies than one without. To a chicken, a maggot is better than ice cream. She requires no minimum wage, hires no lawyers, and doesn't even require a handshake agreement. I can't imagine a better partner. You can throw out the stinkiest, nastiest kitchen scraps and she attacks them as fervently as kids going for mac 'n' cheese. I can't imagine a functional farm without a flock of chickens. If we tried to pay someone to do what these ladies do it would bankrupt us in a month. They work all day, never complain, never get drunk, go to bed when the sun goes down—what's not to love?

Now to the pig. Two pigs can eat as much stuff as a few dozen chickens. If you have a lot of garden scraps, dairy waste, or orchard rubbish, a couple of pigs can keep things tidy while growing bacon. Ahhhh, bacon. And lard. Need I say more?

Isn't it interesting that in the days before modern mechanization and cheap fuel the most efficient way to raise pork was with skim milk? Cream has always been valued, at least until the government experts told us to replace butter and lard with hydrogenated vegetable oil. Before Americans became fixated on debilitating no-fat diets, cream was foundational to nutritious foods. The herbivore (dairy cow) could turn cellulose into milk, which separated into cream and skim milk. Before extremely modern days, skim milk wasn't considered nutritious enough for humans to eat. Feeding it to pigs, though, yielded bacon, ham, sausage, and lard. Talk about alchemy.

Of course, in addition to eating almost anything, pigs have a plow on the end of their nose. Two pigs in a portable pen (we called ours the Tenderloin Taxi) can turn grass into garden spots. In the past, we've run a 6 ft. X 8 ft. hinged pig pen containing two pigs down through the winter chicken quarters. With all four corners hinged, the pen can be moved forward each day by one person walking it like a parallelogram. One side, then the other, then back to the first side. In about three goes it's completely moved. The pigs dig deeper than the chickens and keep the bedding uncapped and fresh. Sometimes they even bring up a few earthworms for chicken treats.

We use pigs to aerate our bedding under the cattle. We call them pigaerators. The sheer petroleum, machinery, and driving time it would take to do this without pigs is enormous. Pigs do it for fun; we don't have to drive them, start them, fix them, or drain their oil. They gain value while doing all this work, unlike machinery, which depreciates. If you throw up an electric fence around a bramble patch and feed them on the thorns, they'll root out the nasty briars and turn it into nice pasture. To do that with human labor and machinery seems barbaric and wasteful. Technology has nothing on a pig.

How about sheep and goats? We use them like a biological weed eater around the farmstead and in the outer fields. With electric netting, we can create any configuration imaginable and move these critters from spot to spot. Sheep and goats eat everything they can reach, leaving behind marvelous nutritious droppings for earthworms and soil microbes. They strip off every thorn from thistles. They wade happily into multi-flora roses and completely defoliate them.

In fire-prone areas many landowners now pay for sheep and goats to control biomass in order to prune without bringing in a fire-risky engine and whirling blade that could hit a rock and cause a spark. Fire control with sheep and goats is gaining popularity in arid urban areas, providing a whole new entrepreneurial opportunity for modern farmers.

That these small animals relish weeds, seeds, and brush is almost miraculous if you stop and watch them. Their little frenetic lips wrap around the tiniest morsel and with dainty but voracious action reduce tangled vegetation to open spaces. I find this work mesmerizing to watch. And if I don't have time to watch it, I know it's ongoing while I write this article or read a good magazine like *The Mother Earth News*.

Finally we come to the queen: the cow. I've left her for last because she is the most finicky. She doesn't scratch like a chicken or dig like a pig, but she can turn mountains of biomass into luscious nutrition: meat and milk. "But she's wasteful," the anti-cow crowd cries. Well of course she's wasteful; that's why the best soils on the planet developed under mega-fauna and specifically, large herbivores. Africa's Serengeti, South America's pampas, Mongolia's steppes, America's great plains-- all of these soil-rich regions owe their equity to large herbivores.

The fact that the cow excretes 80 percent of what she ingests is the secret to her benefits. No animals puts back more than she IF she's managed according to historical migratory and predatory choreography. Here at Polyface, we call our high tech adaptation of this ancient movement ***mob stocking herbivorous solar conversion lignified carbon sequestration fertilization***. While that may bring on some smiles, it's actually a profound ecological template; the one that has stood the test of time. It's the horse that's won history's ecological races.

Oh, speaking of horses, I almost forgot the horse. I don't have one, but certainly the work horse, whether for cowboy work or draft work, is one of the most valuable animals, at least historically, on the farm.

I could mention others: bison, alpacas, llamas, dogs, cats, rabbits, ostrich, emu, alligator, but I'll run out of space and time. The point I want to make is that the services provided by domestic livestock mimic those provided by wild animals. In addition, these services can be carefully managed for the benefit of the human environment. No animal-less ecology exists on the planet. That in itself should give us pause to realize that they must be fairly important.

The tragedy of our day is that we have divorced these animals and their symbiotic attributers from functional contribution. We've isolated, segregated, confined, and disrespected them in habitat, diet, and function. Doing so inverts their contribution from positive to negative, feeding an unnatural narrative to the anti-livestock folks. That's a shame.

A functional food and farming system is most efficient when it incorporates both plants and animals, in balance, like nature. That we have such wonderful partners to work with us in production, to give us fertilizer, to provide enjoyment and function, is truly a blessing and downright remarkable. So here's to the barnyard group, an assortment of tails, legs, heads, feathers and hides that we can love and steward while they in turn take care of us. I call that win-win.

25

Mutual Interdependence
written in 2018

Do-it-yourself and self-reliance life themes are wonderful . . . to a point. Questioning DIY themes in a homestead-styled publication may seem heretical, but I'm going to pursue a secondary idea: building community relationships.

Every movement runs the risk of becoming cultish, or at least over-running its original objectives. Animal welfare morphs into militant animal worship. Concern about genetic diversity morphs into demonization of everything except heirloom seeds and breeds. Eating less meat morphs into militant veganism.

Reactionary pendulums never stop in balance; they swing wildly to the opposite side, eventually demanding correction to balance the over-correction. When we rebel against citified Hot Pocket convenience-dependency, we can easily fall prey to a cumbersome lonely tiring farmstead independence that eventually wears thin.

I propose a balance called mutual interdependence. A business guru would call this community-based economics. Many times I've had to defend our farm against charges in this vein. "How can you be true blue (one of us) if you buy in grain for your chickens? Shouldn't you be raising it all yourself?" A permutation: "Why don't you farrow pigs? You mean you buy all your weaner piggies?"

Or how about this? "I would never buy chicks from a hatchery. You're not really independent unless you hatch them yourself." Permutations on this theme abound. "Better Boy tomatoes? Tut tut, the only tomatoes to grow are heirloom."

How about this one? "Why do you have a tractor? You should be using draft power because they make babies and don't require diesel fuel." An ancillary idea: "You should not use an ATV to get around. You should use pedal power only."

Here's the real kicker: "I don't want employees; I don't want partners; I don't want anybody around. People steal from you, take advantage of you; they're ornery and just a bother. I'm going to do it all myself."

Energy enters the fray too. "Why do you have propane hovers for brooding your chicks? Do you use solar electric fence energizers? Why aren't you making bio-diesel? Why are you still hooked into the grid?" Now don't get me wrong. I'm jazzed about all alternative energy but I'm not an engineer and don't enjoy tinkering with laboratory infrastructure and multi-testers. I'm not good at any of that.

I'm really good at pasturing cows and poultry, working in the woods, building compost and telling stories. So that's what I do. Anyone keeping up with successful business principles knows about the StrengthsFinder platform. The basic premise is that rather than overcoming our weaknesses, we get much farther by leveraging our strengths and building a team with complementary gifts.

Knowing what we're not good at is as important as knowing what we're good at. Frittering away a day on a project that's frustrating and not enjoyable means we've just missed two opportunities. The first is to do another project that is within our strength, where our time is far more effective. The second is that we have denied someone who loves what we don't from expressing their gift, or showing off their talent.

Many times the constraint on collaboration is as much economical as emotional. We don't have the money to pay for help, so we waddle through the project mumbling and stumbling. If successful outfits have anything in common it is the ability to develop functional teams.

In the self-reliance literature, I see a lot about gardening, solar energy, food preservation, spinning and survival techniques, but I see practically nothing about building strong collaborative teams. Gurus who achieve ultimate independence on their own are abnormal. They become gurus because they are highly unusual.

Most of us do better with some help. Rugged individualism and "I did it my wayism" might work for some things, but for most, collaborative teamwork gets us where we want to go faster and more enjoyably. Determining what to do ourselves and what to farm out to helpers is a critical skill to make our farmsteads sing. It starts with an honest and soul-level assessment of our strengths: what we love, what we're good at, and what we know something about.

If it doesn't fit there, chances are we'd do better practicing some mutual interdependence. Just to stimulate the thought juices, here are a dozen things we invest in to make our farmstead run more effectively:

1. **Hiring front end loader work.** Unless you're putting more than 500 hours a year on your tractor, it's probably better not to own one and hire a neighbor. Farmers work cheap. Back when we were getting started (we now have several tractors with front end loaders) we hired a neighbor with a front end loader for just $25 an hour—that included the equipment and driver. Pretty cheap.

2. **Slaughter experts for large animals.** In the early years, Dad and I slaughtered 6 beeves one fall. We thought it was a way to save money. But we could only do two a day and then had to drive them over to the butcher to get them cut up, a round trip of 30 miles. The next year we paid them to do it and we watched as two guys slaughtered one every 15 minutes. Dad looked at me and said: "We'll never compete with that." We haven't done one at the farm since.

3. **Milk cow.** Growing up, we always milked a couple of Guernsey cows. But selling milk was illegal and selling chickens wasn't, so we got rid of the cows and raised chickens. Today, we contract with a young guy to milk our two cows. We still get the raw milk, but we aren't doing it ourselves and we're just paying a service fee.

4. **Hauling cattle.** We have a couple of cattle trailers, but when we need to move several hundred from one property to another, we hire a couple of retired guys in the community who have nice big trucks and trailers. They charge by the loaded mile and it's a good deal compared to us ether being inefficient or capitalizing additional equipment. Unless you're needing a trailer two days a week, you probably shouldn't own one. The

neighbor you use might become a friend.

5. Delivery driver. I don't like to pound the pavement. I don't like to go to town. But I know that's where our customers are and we need to serve them. So we hired a delivery driver; best investment ever and worth every penny. I get to stay home and produce while he fights with urban traffic and finds a place to park. He enjoys that and I enjoy working on the farm; both of us are happy.

6. Sales agents. Few farmers enjoy making sales calls. I don't mind it, but it detracts from my real passion, which is working on the production end and innovating new land healing techniques. And watching earthworms proliferate. So we pay a commission for a couple of folks to make sales calls. I hope they become millionaires. If they do, they'll drag me along with them. In general, adding a sales commission on your products will not overprice them. Furthermore, a sales agent telling potential customers about your best tomatoes in the world is less self-aggrandizing than you saying it about yourself.

7. Mechanic. Unless you love working in the shop, build a good relationship with a couple of community mechanics. Sure, you need to do rudimentary things to not be completely dependent on others, but don't lose your salvation and marriage over a repair job. Take it to town and go plant some more potatoes that you can sell to pay for the repair bill.

8. Bookkeeper. Few farmers, including this one, enjoy financial paperwork. We love breeding records, grazing records, planting records. But financial records? Yuck. Every community has good ones; ask around and find one you can trust, then let it go.

9. Excavation. Sure, you can buy a used bulldozer or track loader, sometimes for under $15,000, but do you know how to operate it? Here on our farm, we do a lot of farm tractor front end loader work. But when it comes to building a pond or scraping off a pad for a structure, we don't even think about doing it ourselves. We have a guy in the community that can pick your nose with a track loader; no way in the world you'll ever compete with his skill. A good operator can do the job cheaper than you by the time you buy and maintain your machine and then recuperate from turning it over on yourself.

10. Web design. Some people love figuring all this stuff out. Others don't. Lots of e-skill is out there. Use it. And go sell five more pigs to pay for it. On the other hand, if e-design floats your boat, offer your services to a farmer friend. Maybe that farmer will trade you milk for e-work.

Obviously I have my own biases, transparently noted above. This list will not be yours, but make a list. Write down what you really would do if time or money were not an issue, then figure out how to finagle help for everything else. It'll make your farmstead sing and might even save your marriage.

26

Incrementalism

written in 2018

My dad used to have a saying: "we make haste slowly." He said it tongue in cheek, but the older I get the more I appreciate the wisdom in that. We live in a fast-paced society.

Goodness, everyone seems impatient to me. I seem impatient to me. If a website does not pop up in 3 seconds, I'm gone. I guess I'm average—that's the average time people wait for a website to appear on a screen. Three seconds.

We live in a hurried, harried, frenzied world, trying to cram everything into anything. We relax in a hurry. We work in a hurry. We go to church in a hurry and watch our watches during the sermon. In our luxurious lives, we Americans have more options than any other culture in history. But those options cram our heads with frenzy as we try to take advantage of them all.

Is it any wonder we're doped up on stress relievers? Is it any wonder vacations have become more exotic, more expensive? We say we have to unwind right now, quickly. Yesteryear's simple weddings have become $40,000 affairs that we must work longer hours to afford. All this frenzy pressures us to perform; if not to keep up with the Joneses, at least to keep up with everyone else's "look at me" posts on Facebook

One of my most significant mentors, Allan Nation, founder of *Stockman Grass Farmer* magazine, used to say that "the biological time clock runs at its own pace." In a high tech mechanical world full of technicians and engineers, we're used to making things happen at our pace. But nature often has its own pace; a corollary is that our homesteads have their own pace.

We can sure get tangled up if we try to do everything in a day. People ask me routinely: "Do you use alternative energy? Do you have a root cellar? Do you have a solar cooker?" As the barrage of "do you have" or "do you do" questions intensifies, I find myself becoming apologetic, feeling guilty for not having accomplished more.

We don't do ourselves any favors by bringing our cultural frenzy to our homesteads. Realize that our homesteads reflect not only our passions, but also what's doable with the time, energy, and money at our disposal. A friend asked me the other day if I ever thought about running a food truck. "Every day," I laughed. I have a list as long as my arm of things I'd like to do but haven't . . . yet.

Our farmstead showcases lots of innovations and cool things. But it literally scratches the surface, because the more you do, the more you know, and the more you do and know, the more you realize you could do. Successful development creates inertia toward additional development. This is why we say the homestead is never a destination; it's a journey.

Millennial entrepreneurial business guru Tai Lopez warns his clients not to be concerned about pace, but only be concerned about progress. Confusing the two, or reaching for pace more than progress, derails everything. Remember, the tortoise won the race, not the rabbit.

Sometimes I think we back-to-the-landers can't be satisfied with our own progress. I'm routinely amazed and captivated by projects our tribe gets done; don't let what's undone make you miss relishing the success of wholesome projects. Be content with incremental development. You can never get it all done in a day or a year, so don't be frustrated trying. This is why efficiency gurus preach baby steps. If you don't take the grand vision and break it down into little pieces, you'll never accomplish the grand vision. Or if you do, you'll probably die too soon to enjoy it.

On our farm, we have long-range lists of projects we'd like to do. This is 3-5 years out. We revisit this list every winter during planning sessions to see what should be deleted or amended. For fun, we can go back 20 years and look at those lists. With 20/20 hindsight, they're good for a lot of laughs: "why in the world did we ever think that was a good idea? We were nuts! Glad we didn't do that."

Then we have one year lists. Often those grow out of the 3-5 year lists. As the project continues to be relevant and needful on the long-range plan, it moves up the priority list. Of course, we never get everything done that's on the one year list. Even some of those projects become obsolete or incorrect before we get to them, but not many. The one year group carries a sense of urgency.

Then we make a quarterly list. What has to be done in the next three months? That grows out of the yearly list. Very few changes occur to this list, except to be bumped to the next time frame if we don't get it done. Budgeting for time and projects yields the same benefits as budgeting our financial position.

Seeing what's coming up, emotionally going with the flow of projects written down, creates its own inertia toward urgency. But it's not a panic urgency; it's controlled and deliberate urgency.

Taking this list concept down all the way to daily is beneficial. We even have filler lists. These are projects that take less than one hour. How many times do you finish something and you want to fill some time before lunch or supper or the gravel truck arrives? It's too much time to waste and not enough time to really start onto something significant. A white board posted in a prominent place with a rolling filler list helps you to takes those time niches of the day and use them productively.

Lots of times we use up those few minutes trying to remember what it was that we wanted to do the next time we had a few minutes. It's maddening, isn't it? But with the filler list, we always have those little projects at our fingertips and can jump on them whenever appropriate.

These are techniques to get more done, certainly, but what's more important, they are techniques to turn chaos into order. And to chart progress. On our farm, one of our most enjoyable activities is taking the one-year list during our winter planning sessions and going through it, feeling the gratification of all the completed projects. That satisfaction counteracts the temptation, or tendency, toward feeling like we're not accomplishing anything.

The point here is to enjoy your homestead more than seeing it as something to conquer in a week. Emotional energy drives physical energy, and if we're constantly depressed because we feel like our pace is not fast enough, we'll miss the greatest joy of homesteading, which is seeing progress toward unorthodoxy. The homestead tribe is one that bucks every accepted norm in society. More stuff, more money, more expensive entertainment, more time away from home, more food prepared outside the home, more pharmaceuticals. The list goes on and on.

That's a lot of stuff to buck, folks. Most of us coming to *The Mother Earth News* ideology have some sort of conversion experience, a wake-up moment, that moved us to question whether normal paradigms are correct. That transition is not an immediate thing. Unplugging, do-it-yourselfing, coming home and reducing consumptive footprints all take time to develop. We have to learn not only the path, but new techniques and new ways of living.

So we need to give ourselves a break about our transition speed. "But the sky is falling!" the Henny Pennies scream. In my experience, thoughtful, systematic plodding gets us farther faster than frenetically going after it, ostracizing our kids, alienating our spouses, and scaring everyone around us to death in the process. That doesn't mean we should be wimps about our vision. On the contrary; our resolve should indicate a resoluteness to make changes that most never even realize are necessary.

But smell the roses on the way. Baby steps. Create a priority list. Housing? Fruit trees? Animals? When people ask me what they should grow, I always respond: "Grow what you like first. That includes if you plan to sell it, because you might have to eat your way through the inventory." Often, engineer types make quicker progress on composting toilets, grey water systems, and passive solar development than gardening. That's okay.

Leverage your love and your ability. Don't do first what some guru says should be done first. Do what interests you. That won't guarantee success, but the chances sure are greater. Success breeds success. Some people like to eat the least likeable food items first, on a plate, saving the best until last. Don't do that on your homestead projects. Do the easy ones first. Do the ones you think you can actually do. That success will make you more confident to tackle the ones that currently scare you.

Or, as is often the case, by the time you get to those harder projects, you'll have a few more friends and assembled talent to advise you on the difficult ones. If you're making progress, be satisfied. Most people aren't even doing that. Enjoy the journey, one little incremental step at a time.

27

Be Safe

written in 2018

Farmers have the highest workplace accident rate compared to other vocations. As an older farmer, I have battle scars that put me in that statistical bag. I write this column from personal experience with accidents, both mine and others.

Some 20 years ago a very close elderly farmer friend died in an ATV rollover out in his pasture checking cows. I've ridden ATVs for many years and just this spring, riding very slowly through some tall grass to check the cows, tipped one up on its side and it pinned my leg underneath. Fortunately, my cell phone summoned help. I could have been that statistic.

My worst accident was cutting firewood. You know the saying: "There are old loggers, and bold loggers, but no old bold loggers." I cut a mid-size tree, perhaps 12 inches in diameter, but didn't step away fast enough as it fell. It fell right onto an old stump, which kicked the butt up and whacked me in the face. Concussion, knocked out two teeth, hamburgered my lip and jaw. Very close call. To this day, I don't know why anyone would engage in boxing. That hit to the face was enough for me.

And then I lost the tip of my right pinky when adjusting the chute on the square baler. It buckled as I adjusted the support chains and pinched off the fatty tip of the finger. It doesn't bother me except the shorter finger makes it difficult to catch the P and the shift button when typing.

One of my earliest set of stitches came from a chainsaw accident. Running an old-style 1960s McCulloch with those early bulbous bars, I had a kickback incident that sliced into my shoulder. I knew I'd been cut, but didn't look at it until I got to the house. I went in and asked Teresa to get a band aid so I could go on out and finish—I was in a hurry because we were leaving the next day on a trip.

When I took my hand away and looked at it, I nearly fainted. Looking into that deep incision, at my own white meat, wasn't too appetizing. We learned something that day: when you walk into the hospital emergency room and say "chainsaw" they don't make you wait. It was just bad enough to scare the living daylights out of me, but not bad enough to hit any tendons or bone.

These are injuries that actually happened. Numerous others were close calls, where I walked away, but could have been killed. The first significant one was when I was in my late teens and mowing some hay. A groundhog caught my attention. I quickly stopped the tractor, hopped off to dispatch him, and to my horror watched the tractor roll down the hill, over a cliff, through some trees, and land in a creek. Fortunately, the tractor was unharmed but the mower needed some serious repairs.

Farm accidents occur because of four basic issues.

1. Inexperience. Knowing the limitations of a machine, what can happen as a result of an action, how an animal will respond—all of this is a skill. Acquiring any skill takes repetition. That's the foundation of mastery.

Anyone can jump on a tractor and put it in gear and drive down the lane or out through a field. But skill requires driving the tractor in snow, in rain, on a hill, uphill, down hill, side of a hill, pushing something, pulling something. You get the idea. And you can't Google experience. All you can do is repeat, repeat, repeat, in different conditions.

How much can you put on a trailer before it's overloaded? What does "park on the level" mean? A few close calls are necessary to instill a respect for limitations. Invincibility may be a good character quality for soldiers, but it's death for farmers. Knowing when a situation is unsafe requires being in a lot of different situations.

One of my rules is to always park the truck or tractor for a quick get away. When I work in the woods, I always turn around and park so that I can jump in and go if something happens. If the ground is slick, always park facing downhill so you won't be stuck. Don't get yourself in a tight spot.

Knowing what a tight spot is means you've been in a few. If you're a novice, think ahead before turning off the engine. Realize that you will probably get yourself in a tight spot due to ignorance; carry a cell phone in order to summon help. The problem with tight spots is that we feel stupid for having gotten ourselves into them so in order to not make it public, we try to be heroic and extricate ourselves by ourselves. And that's when something rolls over on us. Don't be heroic; call for help. That's a lot cheaper than a funeral.

2. Speed. Just like deaths on highways, speed kills on the farm too. Remember I said when I cut my shoulder with the chainsaw, I was in a hurry because Teresa and I were going away the next day? That frenzy coupled with thoughts of being elsewhere absolutely created the accident. Had I been more methodical, more in my normal rhythm, I'm confident I wouldn't have caught the tip of the chainsaw on an adjoining tree.

Slow down when you're in a ticklish situation. And that doesn't mean slipping the clutch without changing gears. One of the single biggest lessons I teach to our farm interns is that when backing something with the tractor, throttle back, drop to first gear, and take your time. Revving the engine and staying in 4th gear reverse is not the way to back the manure spreader into the barn.

3. Improper maintenance. Axes, hatchets, chainsaws, knives, hoes, and mattocks—all edges—need to be sharp. When they're dull, you have to apply more force, and that force is what makes things glance off or break. A chainsaw should pull itself through the cut; if it doesn't, sharpen it. If you're cutting meat or processing chickens, a dull knife is an accident waiting to happen.

From lubrication to putting the little check clip in the hitch pin, properly maintained equipment, tools, and machinery are much safer than thrown together halter-skelter in make-do hurry-up. Sure, there's a place for duct tape, baling twine, and some number 9 wire. But working brakes, sound sledge hammer handles, and Power Take Off (PTO) guards are life savers.

4. Distraction. On our farm, we prohibit ear buds and texting during work hours. Why? Because inattention is deadly. You can't hear the funny noise in the hay mower. You can't hear the stampede of cows coming behind you. In military training, recruits learn "situational awareness."

You cultivate this by looking up and out, not down and fogged in. In our highly techno-gadgeted world now, this is a serious problem. We watch screens and look at keyboards—tiny ones, even on watches. The smaller our screens get, the less aware we are of our surroundings.

On the farm, situational awareness means keeping your feet out from under the trailer hitch when you unhook. It means knowing which cow in the herd has an attitude and which one doesn't. It means keeping your fingers out of places where you could lose one. Hold a chisel or punch with a pair of channel lock pliers, not your fingers. Think about what happens if the hammer misses.

Never, ever, ever reach into a PTO-powered machine when an operator is on the tractor. It's too easy for the tractor driver to get impatient and engage the PTO or hit something else, from hydraulics to gear shift, while you're back there finagling with the stuck hay or clogged spreader beaters. If you're not the one driving, tell the driver to get off before you stick your hands in there. That's situational awareness.

Now for a parting shot: on our farm, everyone must have earplugs on their person at all times. I don't start a tractor without putting in earplugs. Or a chainsaw. Wear a hard hat whenever you're working in the woods. My hard hat has protected me from numerous concussions over the years. And don't ever wear ball cap hats; wear wide brimmed hats to keep the sun off your ears and neck. My wonderful neighbor, Jim, died from skin cancer that started around his ears and neck from years spent unprotected from the sun. As soon as the melanoma started, he switched to wide brimmed hats, but it was too late. He was 30 years older than I and I hope I switched in time.

Don't store your gasoline next to the welder. Some 90 percent of all barn fires are caused by rat-chewn electrical wires and dust. When I read that statistic, I ripped all the electricity out of our barn. When we need power at the barn, we run a heavy extension cord. If you need light at night, use an LED lantern. Keep a fire extinguisher in the shop. Watch where you step and stay rested . . . so you can think about where you step. Don't become another farm fatality. The tomatoes need you.

28

Travel Eating

written in 2019

Since I'm now traveling 120 days a year—roughly a third of the time, which is all I can stand—people routinely ask me how I handle eating on the road. I'm actually writing this column while traveling on a speaking gig in New Hampshire. In fact, I do much of my writing away from home these days. I wrote my last two books on airplanes. But back to food.

First, a disclaimer. I don't have all the answers. All I can do is share what works for me, realizing that I'm a solidly built—a euphemistic way to say I trend toward weight—over-60-year-old geezer. This is to say that my metabolism has slowed considerably since teenage years. That is a blessing and a curse. The blessing is that I can easily deprive myself of food and the curse is that I can put on weight easily. I'd make a great brood cow—eating rag weeds and staying slick and fat. I did not get the tall and slim gene.

With that in mind, the first answer to the question is that I fast. Fasting is good for most of us. The three-meal imperative is actually quite uncommon historically. Eating times are highly cultural. Most of us are actually social eaters:

when someone is eating, we want to join them. If nobody is around, it's easier to just do something else during the time we'd be eating.

For the record, I hate eating alone. I'd rather fast than eat alone. So if I'm at a hotel and the plan from my client is to eat breakfast before he picks me up for the day's activities, I'll often not eat anything rather than sit alone at a table. Over time, I've concluded that sleep is far more important than food, which makes it emotionally easy to skip a meal if it means I can get another hour of shut-eye.

Actually, fasting sharpens my senses and keeps me from being sluggish. I got onto this in college when I was on the debate team and we'd travel all over the southeast to debate tournaments at other colleges. Never fully prepared for these tournaments, we'd cram our speeches and evidence to the last minute. I remember the first time I went 36 hours without eating, preferring to work on my case rather than eat. I brought home a nice big trophy that time and never looked back.

I appreciate that "not eating" is an unacceptable answer for most. And my lovely bride of 38 years, Teresa, at this point of the explanation smiles and adds: "now you see why I don't like traveling with him." So yes, I'm a party pooper on traveling and eating. I belabor the point because I think it's a first viable idea on handling food during travel. The first way to preserve integrity and authenticity in our eating can be to simply fast, especially if it's a short trip. If Teresa does come with me on a trip, everything I've just said comes off the table, pun fully intended.

When I walk through the airport concourse and look at the food options, nothing appeals to me. Oh, that's not to say I'm not hungry and would love to chow down on something, but my food snobbishness hinders me from participating in the choices on offer. Fasting lets me get more work done on my laptop and keeps me from patronizing establishments that harm the earth. And no, I've never played solitaire on my laptop. I use this puppy for my workaholic lifestyle.

Even at home I've cultivated kind of a two meal a day regimen and really like it. Just an apple or a slice of cheese between times works fine. Many people now practice almost a daily 18-hour between meal regimen known as mini-fasts. Okay, enough of this horrible deprivation idea.

What the fasting allows, though, is a higher probability— and budget—to seek out and enjoy integrity food wherever it is. Fortunately, it is much more available than it was many years ago. Even some airports now carry locally-sourced farmers' market type fare. Not many, but some.

Smoothies can be quite satiating and easy on the traveler. A Naked Juice or Odwalla smoothie takes the edge off and acts as a bridge until something more substantial can be found. As soon as you break the 3-meal cult, lots of options open up, and I think that's my main point here. Traveling already breaks the home routine; just enjoy it and push the limits of what's not routine. You might enjoy it.

In this regard, I'm reminded of the story an organic produce grower told me about traveling with a livestock farmer friend to a sustainable farming conference. They were getting famished and finally decided to stop at the next available place as long as it wasn't a McDonald's. They came upon a diner and went in. The produce grower purchased a hamburger with no lettuce and tomato. The livestock fellow purchased a Ceasar salad with no meat or poultry. They both refused to buy the industrial counterpart of what they produced, opting instead to buy the industrial option they didn't know. Sometimes that's just the way it is.

Which brings me to the next main point: preparation. I know people who travel—in cars—with more food than luggage. When we travel in a car, we take stuff to eat. Sandwiches, apples, nuts, jerky or dehydrated fruit are all great options. We try to avoid stuff with a lot of crumbs and juice. Apples are much better than oranges, for example. Dried apricots are better than popcorn, which gets into every crevice of the car seat and soils your pants with butter stains. Been there, done that.

My favorite flying companion is jerky or meat sticks. It's ideal because it's not crumbly and packs a huge punch with little volume or weight. Jerky swells up inside of you and offers lots of high nutrition from a little bag. Dried fruit, from apple slices to raisins to apricots are the non-meat counterpart. But ditto for the volume. Once all that gets inside you and your body handles two or three apples' worth of food, you can have other problems while traveling. Never use traveling as a time to experiment with your body's tolerance level for assimilation. Don't do it.

Nuts work well, but be careful. They're heavy on the stomach and can quickly make you feel sluggish. That's not what you want if you're making a presentation. Nuts do travel well and are easy to eat on the fly. The point here is that pre-thinking flight times, meal itinerary, and activities can help identify the eating holes and how much you need to take to fill in around those valleys.

In the end, though, regardless of fasting and planning, sometimes my body is screaming for something to eat. Maybe I'm flying international and can't bring any food items through customs and I have a long layover. All sorts of scenarios exist where my above protocols break down. So what next? If I have to buy food, I look for something unprocessed, something simple. Soup. Clam chowder. Corn chowder.

A lot of this is knowing your own body. Each of us is different, and what works for me might not work for you. I love bread, but bread doesn't love me. It hangs around, if you know what I mean. Believe it or not, the paleo movement has now made it not too weird to get a burger with no bun or condiments. Drink water. Don't get pizza. Fresh squeezed juice is okay as a beverage. Pricey, but remember, if you don't eat but one meal a day (that's my preference when I'm traveling) you can afford to spend a bit more on good stuff . . . once.

Get an egg fried for breakfast, not a McMuffin. I avoid the fast food franchises like the plague. In Charlotte, you can get pulled pork barbecue without a bun. All that said, everyone has a weakness. Mine is ice cream. Yes, I know where the gelato stand is at Charlotte.

Don't anybody think I'm a traveling ascetic. Yes, I have my limits and protocols, but it's okay to indulge occasionally too. I like the 80/20 rule. It's a business axiom that applies to many things, but I use it to avoid being a food cultist. Eat 80 percent right and you can handle 20 percent not right. Most Americans eat 100 percent wrong, even at home. So an 80/20 mix of right and wrong is close enough, gives a little forgiveness in the choices, and even lets us indulge in a Snicker's bar once in a while. Wearing food snobbery on your sleeve can get old.

The main thing is to think it through, experiment for what works for you, keeping you healthy and sharp, and don't veer too far away from your body's normal ingestion, except for fasting. That is the only major deviation that seems to have no ill side effects. Happy traveling.

Interns

written in 2019

Interns are not cheap help. For all the things they are, they not cheap help. The only people who think internships are exploitive have never had interns. To be sure, some mentors are better than others and some farms are better than others, but generally interns get a fair return on investment. How else can anyone learn this much this fast with so little investment?

Here at Polyface, we've been doing a formal mentor/ intern program for nearly 25 years and are familiar with many other programs from which we've learned a thing a two. Not everything, to be sure, but a lot of things.

Internships are the ultimate hands on, learning-by-doing educational option, dating back to some of the earliest instructional models recorded in human history. It's a long and proud legacy. At our farm, we make a distinction between apprentices and interns. Interns come for five months: May 1-Sept 30. Apprentices are like graduate school; they come out of the interns and stay another year, Oct. 15-Oct. 15.

Internship is boot camp. Apprenticeship is officer training school. I wrote a book about apprenticeships, but in this column I want to hit the key elements of a successful program.

1. Be ready to teach and be ready to learn. Mentors must be apt to teach, must enjoy questions about everything because interns will probe every facet of life: where you go to church, what kind of car you drive, how you picked the names for your kids. Nothing is off the table. This is an intimate relationship and it's like having adult kindergarteners running around wanting to know everything about everything. For interns, the key attitude is to assume you don't know anything and that every single step, word, and gesture from the mentor has meaning. The goal is to figure out all those meanings.

2. Be formal. The worst intern nightmares are when mentors are lackadaisical about expectations. As my son Daniel says: "Nothing destroys relationships faster than unexpressed expectations." If you expect a certain kind of behavior, language, dress code, spell it out. Nobody can read your mind. Over the years as our farm's application process became more formal, the program became stronger because clear expectations weed out the tire kickers. All the rules act as their own vetting process; if someone can't or won't follow the rules for the application process, he won't follow instructions for watering the chickens.

3. Do check-outs. Never have someone come with all their duds sight unseen or with the idea that "if we like you, you can stay." Occupation is half of ownership. Once they're there, dislodging is difficult. Invite candidates for a couple of days to work, eat, and live with you and then send them home. Make your acceptance or rejection decision after they've gone. If an applicant complains about the cost of coming twice (assuming she gets accepted) that indicates a whiner. If you do some back-breaking grunt work alongside someone for a couple of days, you can gauge their attitude quickly.

4. Formal education is worthless. Over the years, I have found zero correlation between academic success and farming success. In fact, often it's a liability because every problem looks like some sort of focus group issue rather than just going on with it. On the farm, we don't need papers; we need performance. Classroom teaching and practical farm work are not necessarily synergistic; they can be, but it's not guaranteed. We've had interns straight out of the city who don't know a heifer from a pullet, but if their attitude is good, they go right on and do fantastic. During our two-day checkouts, the one key question we ask ourselves is this: am I eager to spend the summer with this person?

5. Live close but not under the same roof. Interns come from varied walks of life and come into the relationship fairly quickly compared to other intimate relationships. It's not a long courtship. But interns revere their mentors. In their minds, proximate living enhances the experience, and it certainly does. But living in the same house is not healthy for either party. The intern-mentor experience is extremely intimate and both parties need time and space to go to their corners. On-farm housing is certainly best, and many exemptions exist for buildings.

In our county, a farmer can build five things without a permit: agriculture building like a barn or shed; something portable, like an RV or a tiny house on a chassis; a treehouse, like Swiss Family Robinson; something that floats, like a houseboat in a pond (yet another reason to have farm ponds); and a hunt camp 900 square feet or fewer. I've seen atrocious and disrespectful housing for interns like tents and chicken houses. Don't do that. Provide some decent space; if you wouldn't live there, don't expect them to; it's just common human courtesy.

6. More enterprises. Certainly some internships are extremely narrow, like learning spinning. But most interns want a variety of experiences. The more enterprises you have going on, the more enticing and more enjoyable the program. Interns get bored quickly so offering new challenges keeps them in a progressing frame of mind.

7. Familial atmosphere. To the intern, the mentor is a guru, which carries an air of distance. The mentor can seem intimidating, and yet openness and inspiration require deep and on-going conversations. The mentor must knock the edge off of this distance. I've seen mentors who won't let interns eat with them, or come into the farm house. That kind of condescending distance does no one any good. At our farm, we eat together for the evening meal. Breakfast and lunch are separate, but coming together at the end of each week day (not weekends) creates down time to talk about the day, plan tomorrow, and just be family. During the summer our farm houses 25 people (10 interns, 2-3 apprentices, staff and families). In order to balance out the summer's educational and relational intensity, we hire a chef for 5 months to do the evening weekday meals and we eat as a family in a large pavilion. While that is a big investment ($10 a plate) it creates a wonderful atmosphere of conviviality.

8. Serious teaching. Interns expect to work, but they also look forward to non work instruction. In our program, we do a monthly lecture, usually on a rainy day, complete with white boards. The interns come with paper, pen, and enthusiastic anticipation. We do field trips to nearby places and make sure everyone gets to the county fair. Like every community, ours has a handful of real experts and we invite them over for dinner and short lecture. Use what's available. Any nature or farming topic is acceptable and most neighbors are eager to come to dinner with a bunch of bright-eyed bushy-tailed young people.

9. Pop quizzes. Again, this may seem trivial, but interns love feeling like they're really in a classroom. Give a reading assignment and then quiz them on it. Add some humor, like Mike's favorite food is _____. Mix in group trivia with serious information they're learning. The competition to get the most right answers is fierce. And yes, two interns is enough to capture the competitive spirit. This is a great way to check progress and stimulate observation—both listening and watching.

10. Set benchmarks. Mentors, or masters, are highly skilled. Repetition is the foundation of skill, but midway through the season sometimes interns can feel like they've already attained enough skill. That's why written benchmarks for different tasks keep interns from complacency. On our farm, we've established benchmarks for lots of things. Moving a chicken shelter: 60 seconds. Putting away 30 dozen eggs: 20 minutes. Eviscerating a chicken: 60 seconds. In my experience, unfortunately, perhaps one in ten interns actually times himself to measure benchmarking. You'd think someone really interested in success would do that, but few do, which speaks to the desire of the intern, not the skill of the mentor.

11. Safety is critical. Situational awareness is one of the key training elements in military special forces. It's just as critical on the farm. Young people from the city, who have never been around cows or machinery often engage in life-threatening behavior. Mentors must think for everyone. And believe me, you can't imagine how creative people can be at lousing something up. This is why instructions must be clear; interns that run off half cocked may end up dead. I have one piece of equipment I do not allow interns to run: a chainsaw. We normally do a session on basic chainsaw operation and I let each one make a couple of cuts just to get the feel of it. But unless someone has a lot of experience running a chainsaw, we keep it off limits. It's just too risky.

12. Balance praise and criticism. Like any close relationship, the mentor-intern one is ripe for misunderstandings and break-down. Moments of bliss inevitably precede moments of frustration. Humans, even in the most perfect circumstances, can say inappropriate things and jump to conclusions that beg forgiveness once the heat of the moment is off. That is why mentors must seek early and frequent opportunities to say "good job." Eventually, dissatisfaction must and will be expressed; some congratulations in the emotional tank will go a long way to preserving an overall equilibrium of trust and appreciation.

Just like a marriage, a lot more is at stake in a successful internship than momentary infatuated hook-ups. You can't over-estimate an intern's ability to tear up equipment, anger a customer, or do some bone headed thing. And you can't over-estimate a mentor's ability to be critical and impatient. This is not an arrangement for the faint of heart. Both must come to the table for the long term and with clear expectations and commitment. Then and only then can it be a mutually enjoyable experience.

30

Faith Farming

written in 2019

Too often in environmentally-themed discussions spiritual reasons for building compost piles and pond dams usually get lost in practical how-to. Our temptation is to get excited about the how, and that's well and good. But if we plan to leave a belief legacy that inspires people to continue building compost piles and pond dams, we need to talk about why.

Business consultants have a search model called "ask why five times." The idea is that you have to ask why that many times before you get to the real nub of an issue. So just for fun, let's do a hypothetical search about compost piles.

Question 1: Why build a compost pile?
Answer: To decompose biomass fast and completely.

Question 2: Why decompose biomass fast and completely?
Answer: Decomposed biomass is the best fertility amendment for soil.

Question 3: Why is compost the best fertility amendment for soil?

Answer: Because that's what feeds the soil's micro-organisms.

Question 4: Why do we need to feed soil micro-organisms?
Answer: Because they are living beings that need feeding.

Question 5: Why do living beings need food?
Answer: Because God made them to eat.

You could find fault with my progression, but the point is that eventually you end up with big questions about creation, why we're here, and what's the point of it all. Certainly you could be a fatalist, atheist, or agnostic, but ask why enough times and you will get beyond Hollywood and Candy Crush. You'll get to bedrock values and beliefs.

When people ask me why I farm the way I do, my favorite response is "because it's right." That's obviously a moral statement. It supposes that if somebody farms differently, it could be wrong. And what is ultimately right and wrong is based on a code of ethics outside the human psyche.

Interestingly, the faith community—especially the conservative element—on the whole espouses a different view of earth stewardship than I do, even though we may read the same scriptures. That's where my "because it's right" bears special significance. A fellow church-goer whose vocation is promoting chemical fertilizers, genetically modified corn, and factory farming quickly justifies these activities based on a dominion mandate. When that is the operative word, you can be sure it's not about nurturing and caressing; it's about being a Conquistador. Indeed, God has been invoked throughout history for plenty of atrocities.

As a teenager in a conservative Christian home during the Vietnam era and the launch of *The Mother Earth News*, hippies, and Woodstock, I lived a strange dichotomy. Our church friends routinely panned health food and compost as an outgrowth of tree hugger earth muffins. Our farm friends talked about Gaia, compost, free love and coming back to the land.

In our family, the two worlds were not exclusive. We were not hippies, but we deeply appreciated the earth care theme they brought to the table. Unlike our church friends, we found shared values with our hippie friends in the arena of earth care. Why must these two worlds be mutually exclusive? Through that experience and the years since, I have not found the earth care community contradictory to my Biblical worldview; I have found it complementary in many ways.

In fact, if I could state my belief succinctly today, it would be this: the entire physical creation is an object lesson of spiritual truth. In other words, God needed a way to illustrate what humanly we could not see. That profound idea frames how I farm in remarkable ways.

For example, forgiveness is a big spiritual principle. What does forgiveness look like? It looks like healthy animals and plants when all around sickness rules. It looks like green grass when drought sucks moisture out of the soil. It looks like filling ponds when all around flood waters invade the neighborhood. It looks like simple infrastructure easy to rebuild after the devastation of a tornado. Each of these examples has a counterpart visible in orthodox industrial farming, which depletes water, decreases immune function, and creates monolithic buildings hard to rebuild after disaster.

The point is that I want visitors to our farm to leave exclaiming to themselves: "Wow, so that's what forgiveness looks like."

Let's take another example: neighborliness. Most people know the golden rule: "Do unto others as you would have then do unto you." It's pretty simple, but again, what does that look like? What does being a good neighbor really mean? It sure doesn't mean stinking up the neighborhood and polluting the aquifers. It doesn't mean pesticide drifting across the boundary fence or errant promiscuous genetically modified organisms invading your neighbors' fields.

According to Biblical narrative, the highest commendation after this physical existence is "well done, you good and faithful servant." What does faithfulness look like? It has to do with stewardship of gifts, beliefs, and God's stuff. Or course, to the Christian everything we see is God's stuff. "The earth is the Lord's" the Psalmist proclaims. Faithfulness, then, is fidelity to all that God has entrusted to our care, from our spiritual awareness and growth to caring for God's stuff. And I don't say "God's stuff" as a trite phrase; it's pretty serious business to be entrusted with somebody's possessions, especially God's.

That's not something to be taken lightly. In God's economy, then, how do we illustrate faithfulness to help us comprehend unseen tenets like doctrine and spiritual growth? I'd say we show it by how we care for His physical creation. In other words, our footsteps and efforts should leave behind more soil, more breathable air, more drinkable water, more conscious awareness of how ecology works, more awe regarding the mysteries of life. That means we think about actinomycetes as much as we do about picking praise songs for Sunday worship, don't you think? It means that nothing is outside the sphere of spiritual interest.

It means that we appreciate all that microbial life, those 7 billion critters in a double handful of healthy soil upon which we all depend. Indeed, realizing that the visible is completely dependent on the invisible is another profound ecological principle with spiritual ramifications. In God's economy, does anyone think a dead zone the size of Rhode Island in the Gulf of Mexico is a good return on investment? Or the fact that 200 years of European occupation in my Shenandoah Valley of Virginia yielded 3-5 feet of top soil erosion? Is that a good ROI?

The fact that during all that time good Lutherans, Baptists, and Presbyterians were taking the cash from eroding fields and putting it in offering plates to help missions projects around the world simply heightens the obvious hypocrisy of divorcing the spiritual-physical union. The ultimate segregated thinking is when we separate the two, as if one has moral dimensions and the other one doesn't.

We have room for one more object lesson: whosoever will. Even the non-religious, if they've ever darkened the door of a Sunday School, will be familiar with the most famous Biblical verse, John 3:16, where "whosoever will" is the dominant theme of Christ's sacrifice and God's grace. What does whosoever will look like?

In farming, I would suggest that it looks like a system in which entry is easy. If you want to grow a chicken for Tyson, the first thing you have to do is build a half million dollar foot-ball-field-sized factory house. Would you call that an impediment to entry? I sure would; in fact, I'd go so far as to say it's elitist. If you need to put in half a million dollars to join the fraternity, that's pretty tough.

Compare that with pastured poultry, using mobile, modular shelters. On our farm, we can build these brand new for $300. That's pocket change in today's economy. All you have to do is not go to the movies a few times and you have enough to build one and be in the chicken business. That's a "whosoever will" model; anyone can get in. Plenty of people raise pastured poultry on land they don't even own because it fits nicely with other enterprises, like under orchard trees or along with cows. The physical empowerment such a model offers is like the spiritual empowerment that whosoever will offers: poor, rich, smart, stupid, wise, foolish. All are welcome. If you have to grow 20 tons of tomatoes in order to access the market, that's pretty restrictive. But if you sell to your neighbors or at farmers' markets, you can get in with a couple of plants. That's "whosoever will."

Plenty of other spiritual concepts can be illustrated by our farming, and I've done that in my book *The Marvelous Pigness of Pigs: Caring for All of God's Creation*. I can't imagine being a conventional orthodox chemical-based factory farmer living under the tension of contradictory values. Dare we ask: does what we believe in the pew show up on the menu? That's the question for farmers and all eaters. Too often, the great spiritual truths espoused from the pulpit never nestle into the fields and forks of practice.

Harmonizing our spiritual and physical universe is one thing. Caretaking our physical world out of our spiritual understanding is even better. I covet the day when the faith community embraces creation stewardship mandates as practically and profoundly important as spiritual principles. They are one.

31

Farm Training
written in 2019

"Where do I go to learn this stuff?" is a common question aspiring farmers and homesteaders ask. A quick and easy answer is "attend a *The Mother Earth News* fair." I wish it were really that easy.

To drill down on the question, I'll tell my own training story. Each person's story is different, but threads of commonality exist. That's what we want to tease out. First of all, I started early. I grew up on the farm we operate today. To be sure, my Mom and Dad's off-farm jobs (school teacher and accountant, respectively) paid for the land, but the farm never became what we would call a going concern until my wife Teresa and I married and returned.

The first two threads are to start early and don't worry about the scale or viability of the farm enterprise. Just get involved. I don't think I realized until my late teen years that the farm was not really a business. Oh, we sold some calves at the sale barn but it never actually made a living. I'm sure it made enough to pay the taxes, but not anything close to a salary. It was a great place to grow up, to experiment with different agricultural enterprises, and to develop marketing savvy.

Mom and Dad's situation did not dampen their encouragement for us kids to develop our own enterprises. My older brother raised rabbits and I got my first chickens when I was 10 years old. Sometimes I think my attention to the business of farming makes people think I don't respect non-profitable farms and homesteads. Nothing could be further from the truth. Every enterprise starts from nothing. We're all on some sort of scale, coming from somewhere and heading somewhere else. If our somewhere right now is just a great place to build tree forts, dams in the creek, and plant vegetables, that's fantastic.

The point is to start something, anything, where you are. You can't Google experience. And nothing is more valuable than experience. While you're doing that something, regardless of profit, regardless of scale, you can read, attend seminars, watch videos, attend night classes. I'm a huge believer in doing something practical at the same time that we're doing something academic. They aren't mutually exclusive and they usually fit symbiotically.

Start practicing, anything. You'll learn what you enjoy and what you don't. What you have a knack for and what you don't. For example, very seldom is a person equally adept at plants and animals. We tend to gravitate toward one. How do you know where your gift and heart lie until you play with options?

Sometimes we get fixated on training from somewhere or someone else. As important as that may be, nothing compares to personal experience. I'm sure Michael Jordan had access to the best personal trailers and coaches in basketball, but in his autobiography he says each basket made in a game had 10,000 missed shots behind it. In other words, NOTHING beats experience. The sooner you start, the sooner you start missing baskets, and that's how you learn to make baskets. It's true on the court and it's true in the field.

For sure my greatest mentor was my Dad, whose father (my grandfather) was a charter subscriber to *Rodale's Organic Gardening and Farming* magazine when it first came out in the late 1940s. That was a mainstay around our house. So I stand on big shoulders of the right philosophy, the right world view. Dad and Mom may not have developed an agricultural going concern in their lifetime, but they created the foundation, in thought, practice, and land, for Teresa and I to launch. Never apologize for humble beginnings. And never take launch pads for granted.

Because our family had this environmental ethic, we befriended the eco-farmers in our area and developed close relationships with hippies. As soon as *The Mother Earth News* began being published, it was a mainstay in our home and I remember even as a teenager being mesmerized by the content. So the second big point is to immerse yourself in the literature of your interest. The Plowboy interview in the opening pages of *TMEN* introduced me to Allan Savory, Bill Mollison, Ellie Pruess, A.P. Thomson—all the greats. I didn't have money for travel. But I could do it vicariously through the pages of these illustrious magazines.

Then came books. One of the most valuable investments I ever spent was a fall when I wasn't busy. I was operating a black walnut buying station for Hammons Products Company at the local Southern States dealer. It was a 4-week gig and I had to be there Monday-Saturday 8-5 during October. Most years it was fairly busy, but this particular year the walnuts did not produce in our area and I literally had a couple of folks a day come down with a few sacks. I had agreed to the time and terms, so I took books.

`I read Louis Bromfield, Ed Faulkner, Sir Albert Howard, Phil Callahan, Charles Walters, and the biggest and most favorite, the 1,000 page *The Complete Book of Composting* compiled by the Rodale staff. I underlined, digested, memorized and baptized myself in those pages. They became the backbone of presentations as I began communicating our farm methodology. And of course, I stole plenty of ideas to try on our own farm. But I was armed with the why as well as the how. That one month is still one of the fondest in my memory.

Extremely strapped for money, I could have chafed under the poor walnut crop and wasted time down there sitting on feed sacks in the back doorway of the Southern States store, but instead I invested that time in reading. I think this brings me to a third overall thread: you're responsible for what you know. Goodness, we live in a victim-centric culture where we're encouraged to blame someone else for anything that's askew in our lives.

A friend of mine says that he realized he was an adult the day he decided that his parents had done the best for him that they knew how. Were they perfect? Of course not. But they did the best they knew and he forgave the rest. That's maturity, and the beginning of progress. As long as you think someone else is responsible for your success, your training, your development, you'll be stuck where you are. The day you realize you're responsible is the first day of liberated learning and progress.

Fourth, these friends in the environmental farming and homesteading community that our family began spending time with were all doing interesting and inspiring things. What's the thread? Associating with likeminded people. This means NOT associating with naysayers. Nothing catapults us to try things faster than encouragers; nothing shuts down our momentum faster than people who pooh-pooh our ideas and aspirations.

Businesses now know the value of Mastermind groups. Consider that as part of your training. Surrounding yourself with people as or more competent than you challenges you to try harder and do better. If you spend your time with whiners and failures you will soon become one. Invest in spending time with people who can teach, mentor, and inspire. Yes, that means working with a farmer you enjoy. For free if necessary. Consider it an investment in your training.

Early on I joined the Virginia Association for Biological Farming (VABF). Trade associations work because they build tribes and communities around practice. The folks who lead these organizations are generally the gurus of their trade. This is all part of rubbing shoulders with the folks who know stuff, and all of us need to rub shoulders with people who know stuff.

This is my story. Today, I think we have far more access to people who know stuff than ever. Often I quip: "I wish I was around when I was young." We have way more information, more seminars, more internships, more conferences. Goodness, we even have YouTube, podcasts and on-line learning. Never has information been more accessible.

The problem is that never before have distractions been as common. Think about all the things vying for our time, from sports to video games to entertainment. Today the average American male 25-35 years of age spends 20 hours per week playing video games. Perhaps this is a good spot to put in things I have never done, which will assuredly place me in the lunatic camp: snow ski, drink coffee, owned a TV, played a video game, visited Las Vegas or Atlantic City, day traded.

If you're going to train to be a winner, it means you can't do everything else. Nobody can do everything. You have to pick and choose. What you put your money and time on defines what you value. How bad do you want it? What could the average American male between 25 and 35 spending 20 hours a week playing video games learn if he devoted himself completely to an interest? Just sayin'.

Life long learning is a practice. I'm learning new things ever day. I still read voraciously. I still get giddy about spending time with an excellent farmer. Excellence is something you cultivate, just like a garden. As financial guru Dave Ramsey notes, we tend to be successful at what we put attention on. Ultimately, training to be a successful farmer is just like any other vocational success: experience, information, relationship. Now go grow the prettiest garden around.

32

Business Failures

written in 2019

"What have been your biggest business failures?" It's a question often asked in the afterglow of a can-do go-get'em workshop when everyone feels happy and comfortable enough to explore the not-so-good decisions I've made. Failures don't inspire so I tend not to dwell on them. But they can sure be instructive. Here are my biggest ones over a lifetime of farming.

1. Accounts receivable. My mentor Allan Nation used to say this about being in the food sales business: "It's good because it's a consumable and people have to keep coming back for more; it's bad because you can't repossess yesterday's meal." Truer words were never spoken.

The number one reason businesses fail has nothing to do with product or service; it's cash flow. Just because a venture is profitable does not mean it will cash flow. Money coming in the front door has to be just ahead of money going out the back door.

As farm businesses, we do cartwheels to find customers. When a new patron oohs and aahs over our eggs or tomatoes, endorphin high dulls our senses to the harsh reality that praise and gratitude do not pay the bills. Those grateful customers need to pay because all the platitudes in the world won't make us economically viable.

Since we're desperate for a sale, though, we don't dog the slow pay. We want to believe the best in people. After all, they love our product. So we put off the difficult conversation. We're struggling; they're struggling. If we act hardnosed, then we're not being empathetic enough. You know the story; it's been told a million times. Extending credit and letting accounts receivable build up is much easier than being perceived as mercenary and unloving. But that easy path leads to financial ruin.

Until you have a track record of trust with a customer, keep everything on a pay-today status. Once you have a year of good relations under your belt, then a net 30 days is okay. Because those of us in the integrity food space inherently deal with more startups, we're more vulnerable to shady business characters. And yes, the worst offenders are often either deeply religious or farm-to-table friends. Sad, but true. Keep your accounts receivable short.

2. Fit of client or partner. When you're developing a business relationship, whether it's a partner, employee, collaborator or any other pairing, you must be mindful of the three C's outlined by business guru Simon Sinek: character, culture, community. Every business has these three distinctive elements and any time we work with people that violate any of these C's, we regret it.

Entrepreneur guru Tai Lopez says the number one business mistake he's made over the years is not firing someone soon enough. Once you start having this gnawing feeling, misgivings about your future relationship, the prudent thing is to cut and run. Trying to fix a situation that doesn't fit your character, culture, or community is not worth the energy. Rubbing shoulders routinely with folks who sap our emotional energy is a nightmare.

You don't have to be nasty about it; just explain that it doesn't fit. We rented a property from a lady who died two years into a five-year lease. When the three children (who were in their 50s) took over, we found ourselves in the midst of a family squabble. Instead of trying to help them work it out, we should have walked away the first time we smelled the rat. Ditto another landlord who wanted his pastures to look like a golf course. We're not in the golf course business. We walked away from that one part way through the agreement.

We had an apprentice who came to me one morning about 9 months into his 12-month deal with this announcement: "I think I've learned everything I need to know." I responded quickly: "Well then you'd better leave by tomorrow morning before you forget it all." Poor partnerships are far worse than no partnerships. When it starts to smell bad, don't try to salvage it. It's not worth the effort. Part company and move on.

3. Fast growth. Trends reach credibility over time. A one season statistic does not a trend make. For a couple of years we were extremely short of eggs so we offered a fellow the opportunity to grow eggs for us. We built him a portable hen house on skids and raised 1,000 pullets for him. We guaranteed him so much per dozen and the eggs began rolling in. If we had expanded by only 400, we probably would have been fine.

But we had overestimated the market and couldn't grow it fast enough to accommodate the over-rapid expansion. This flock added 400 dozen a week. We ended up paying him $10,000 for eggs we fed to the pigs. Not good.

If a market opportunity presents itself, of course you want to jump on it. But over-running your headlights, as my dad used to say, is not wise. Better to be short in inventory than long and throw stuff away. The problem with direct marketing is that if you produce one egg beyond your market, its value is zero. The commodity market is big enough to absorb growth as fast as you want to bring it. If you add 5,000 acres of corn to the commodity market, prices don't change and someone will always take it. But if you make one too many bags of cornmeal flour for muffins, it's expensive chicken feed.

Don't worry about speed. Just worry about trajectory. The hare loses; the tortoise wins. As long as your movement is progressing the way you want to go, don't get frustrated with speed. Just enjoy the ride however fast it goes.

4. Commodity misfit. Many years ago I had to replace several hundred yards of a boundary fence in the edge of the woods. The trees on our side of the fence were massive and growing toward the pasture (daylight) on the neighbor's side. I figured if I was going to invest the time and money in replacing the fence I might as well harvest the big trees overhanging from our side not only to protect the fence but also to make some money in logs.

Working with just a saw and a tractor, I spent free time in the winter pecking away at the project and finally finished. I didn't have any way to haul the logs to the sawmill but I knew a fellow who had a log truck with a knuckle boom loader. I called him and he agreed to load the logs and take them to the mill. When we got to the mill, he set them all out on the yard and a fellow came out of the scale house with a ruler. He told me how many board feet I had, told me the quality of the logs, and told me what the price was.

He wrote me a check and it came within a few cents of paying for the haul fee. I vowed then and there that I would never again take a log to a sawmill. I'd have made more money if I had cut them up for firewood. Some of the knot-free red oaks were veneer quality. What I learned later was that any weathering on the ends automatically marks the log down to "utility." If I had gone along and cut an inch off the ends right before taking them to the mill, I may have doubled my money.

But such are the hidden nuances of the commodity business. Pre-understanding is not for novices; it's for the insiders who run the game. If you're a small outfit, be careful playing footsy with the big boys. They'll eat you alive.

5. Hot shot genetics. Early on in my farming career, I became enamored of genetic development for our cow herd. I tried some artificial insemination and bought a bull that was top of its test group in the state-graded seedstock sale. Well guess what? None of that stock lasted more than a couple of years. Heifers wouldn't breed. They got pink eye. They were completely unacceptable.

I learned that a healthy backwoods animal beats a hot shot industrial stud any time of day. My advice to anyone wanting to upgrade their livestock is to buy solid stock from neighbors and upgrade gently with the kind of bull from the kind of herd you want. The bull or ram is 50 percent of your genetics. Be content with slow improvement; fast genes stall quickly unless you're ready to dump lots of money in crutches like medications, extra feed, and hugs and kisses. The animals have to work for you; not the other way around.

There you have it; some of my biggest business failures. Hope these help you avoid the same ones. That way you can have a different list to share with your grandkids. Keep on keeping on.

33

50 Years of
The Mother Earth News   *2019*

Has it really been 50 years? Indeed, as a 13-year-old in 1970, I remember my strait-laced Christian dad devouring this new magazine, all in black-and-white on rustic paper. It was called *The Mother Earth News (TMEN)* and was filled with every kind of back-to-the-land and self-reliance idea you could imagine. John Shuttleworth steered a visionary team that cranked out a counter-culture issue each month.

Post Woodstock, *TMEN* embodied both the frustration and hope of the first Baby Boomer wave questioning the foundations of the WWII generation. Virtually every icon of the practical environmental movement—and I'm purposely using the word practical to distinguish from radical impractical--enjoyed introductions through the Plowboy interview. Allan Savory, Bill Mollison, A. P. Thomson—each month those of us desperate to re-direct the course of our culture received a bonanza of information and new partners.

What a joy to find a tribe that thought like we did. In those early days, I was but a fledgling teenager raising chickens without vaccines. I even had them on pasture in moveable shelters. As an active 4-Her, I received a steady dose of orthodoxy from the poultry science department at Virginia Tech. In fact, those professors mounted an aggressive campaign to enroll me in their program. They sent me on trips, introduced me to Colonel Sanders (that was memorable) and all sorts of arm-twisting things.

But every time I came home from their activities, there was *TMEN*, a beacon of illumination questioning everything the industrial mechanical orthodoxy said. Its partner, *Organic Gardening and Farming* Magazine, had iconic status in our house, alongside the Bible, which now I realize was quite unusual. We have a saying that you are what you eat, which recently has progressed to you are what you eat eats. A corollary, for sure, is you think what you read. Or you become where you immerse your mind.

In my formative years, *TMEN* was the antidote to conventional establishment-think. It dared to question everything. I remember one especially fascinating story titled "Kon Tipi." The cross-ocean exploits of Kon Tiki were hot at the time, so a title like "Kon Tipi" caught my attention. It was about a homesteading family who built a house in glorified tipi fashion simply using poles and a heavy canvas. The point was that although it would require a new skin in 15 years, the whole structure only cost $5,000. Who can't see the financial value of living in a house that costs $5,000 to rebuild every 15 years? If we all need a house for 60 years, that's 4 builds for a total of $20,000. What's not to love?

This kind of thinking framed my whole perspective of value and cultural norms. Instead of wanting more things, I wanted fewer things. Instead of high capital farming, I wanted low capital farming. Instead of supermarkets I wanted larders, root cellars, and backyard abundance. Then came the Arab oil embargo and the alternative fuels movement took off. Wood, gas, solar, windmills, wood stoves—the pages of *TMEN* each month fueled our minds with alternatives. If I could boil down the magazine's persona to one word during that time it was hope.

Goodness, radical environmentalist Paul Ehrlich—why does anyone listen to him anymore?—predicted the end of oil by the 1980s. We were a decade away from doom. It was easy to be depressed. But *TMEN* served up a steady dose of hope in all sorts of practical alternatives. Who needed anti-depressants when you could dive into *TMEN*'s projects? The can-do spirit pervaded every page.

Undoubtedly, one of the most profound Plowboy interviews in our house was Bill Mollison's introduction to permaculture. I can still recite those foundations of permaculture: stacking, multi-function, high landscape hydration, perennials. That one article made us re-look at all our practices, refining, adding, and developing more resilient systems. Whenever anyone asks what shaped my thinking early on, as an aspiring farmer, *TMEN* receives high marks.

My four-cabinet-file library contains hundreds of yellowed *TMEN* articles on topics as varied as season extension in the garden to cordwood construction to grey water systems. Today, I continue to add to this legacy file. You'd think that everything that could be written about resilient living would have been written by now. But no, innovation continues. So what has changed and what has stayed the same over this half century?

First, as a writer and publisher myself, the obvious advancement is in printing technology. Those early editions were almost glorified newsprint. Today, the glossy four-color look is catchy and first class. For the record, I buy based on content, not on glitzy presentation. But the modern *TMEN* does look cooler on a desk. I'll grant that.

Second, I think the sophistication of the movement's constituency has changed. As the movement and magazine matured, both settled into a less strident critique of everything status quo and realized that not everything normal is bad. Plenty is, to be sure, but not everything. And so *TMEN* found its voice, found a balance and a niche.

As the wild-eyed hippie beaded, bearded, braless free-lovers of the early 1970s matured into parents, employees, and bill payers, the magazine realized that America was not all bad and capitalism helps entrepreneurs. Maybe money per se is not evil. And maybe living in a home that can withstand a snow storm or hurricane is helpful, especially when you have kiddos running around.

I don't think it's uncharitable to say that during the 1990s, *TMEN* struggled trying to re-find and re-define its soul. Circulation plummeted and many of us dropped our subscriptions for a time. I don't know enough about the inner workings and history of the magazine to talk about this transition. All I know is that by the turn of the century, *TMEN* found its footing again, right as baby boomers, who too often got hooked into the grasp of orthodoxy, began questioning it again.

Age has a way of making you rethink where you are, how you got here. In addition to baby boomers rediscovering some of their roots, millenials began asking questions about scarcity, sustainability, and soul-satisfying vocations. Working a lifetime for the corporate man did not provide their parents with soul satiation; growing up in that grind pushed many millenials into social entrepreneurism. And *TMEN* was there to offer hope again.

Which brings me to what has not changed. Practical, how-to advice on wide-ranging topics has been and continues to be the bread and butter of the magazine. But now new understanding into the microbiome, accentuating the soil-health connection, is light years beyond the early fundamental compost building content. A renewed sense of urgency, brought on by millenials' understanding of ecology and hockey-stick graphs, is driving content in these pages.

It's no longer about a more enjoyable way to live, or casting off societal expectations. It's now much more about survival, health, and feeding our grandchildren. My own unscientific observation is that the home schooling movement as well as the whole learning-by-doing educational movement (Waldorf, Montessori, and others) provided a shot in the arm to the methods and mission of *TMEN*. The constituency now is not wide-eyed dreamers; it's reasoned, calculating folks wanting to caress rather than conquer, wanting to explore rather than exploit.

My sense is that the magazine has moved more from a planetary mission to a personal mission. While it's always good to think big and macro, Wendell Berry's admonition that all global problems start with local dysfunction has merit. Crusading about big things somewhere else and castigating people somewhere else doesn't really change the trajectory. Planting a garden, building an energy machine, installing a solarium, creating an herbal stash in our homes—these are things that enable us to participate, viscerally, in the changes we want to see.

Empowerment comes from doing projects that change our situations, where we are now, where we live. Make no mistake, the cumulative affect of multitudinous little things adds up to big changes. That is today's *TMEN* persona. In a day when calamity and dysfunction are on every corner, here is can-do information that moves us from hopelessness to hope. If all we do is concentrate and converse about things beyond our sphere of influence, like Stephen Covey says, we'll eventually wear out, burn out, and descend into depression.

Today's coaching movement illustrates the disempowerment most of us feel. We can't talk to people at businesses; all we get are phone robots. Punch 1, 2, or 3. We can't fix our cars. We can't fix our computers. We can't fix our refrigerators. Everything is complicated and technologically out of our reach. So we have wellness coaches, fitness coaches, nutrition coaches, investment coaches, self-help coaches. You can find a coach for almost anything.

What draws people to the pages of *TMEN* is the same thing that drew us 50 years ago. A despairing sigh of "what can I do" turns into an enthusiastic thousand self-empowering projects in *TMEN* articles. That is a voice that draws all thinking people, all mavericks, all lunatic fringers and I hope *TMEN* offers that clarion call for another 50 years. The future will be interesting and probably quite disturbing, but through these pages we'll all be able to weather the disturbances better.

34

What Animals Teach Us

written in 2020

To all gardeners, this is not a slight against what we can learn from plants. We can learn plenty from them too. But for now, I want to concentrate on what I've learned from a lifetime of raising livestock. I've seen numerous studies showing that working with animals makes people less violent. While that may or may not be true, I am confident it makes us more mindful of how we relate to others.

1. Train early and be serious about it. The longer bad habits persist and the later in life training starts, the harder it is to get control. The smartest farm animal is the pig. In my experience, no animal trains better to electric fence, but no animal tests the fence as much.

When we buy weaner pigs at about 40 pounds, we put them in a solid physical pen and train them to electric fence within a few days of becoming acclimated to their new digs (literally). A portable energizer connected to a short wire 3 feet away from the end of their pen offers a 10,000 volt lesson. As we say around here, "when you're training to electric fence, you want their first experience to be memorable." Don't dilly dally around with half-way voltage. Make it hot.

To keep it consistent during the training period, we put a spring in the middle of that wire to keep it from breaking when the pigs run through it. Without the spring, the pigs would keep breaking the wire every time they went over or under and it would be more of a sideshow—"look, Porky, look at the wire spark"—than a consistent training thread.

Early and aggressive exposure to limits, to fences, to spark, to control expectations creates a lifetime of enjoyment. If you can't go to bed at night knowing your animals will be where they're supposed to be tomorrow morning, you can never really sleep. To be effective, electric fence must be energized sufficiently (this can be a ground rod inadequacy as much as a joules of output issue), tight, visible, and the right height. If any of these is wrong, you'll have issues.

The early and serious certainly works well with people. Children respond to clear, consistent discipline. Teachers must establish clear expectations on the first day of class or they'll be dealing with uncontrollable students the rest of the year. New employees respond to clear and direct rules early. Failure to communicate protocols leaves too much to interpretation, lets bad habits develop, facilitates inappropriate activities, and generally moves an organization into dysfunction.

Too many times I've seen people get animals for the first time and put them in a haphazard pen of baling twine, duct tape and half rotten pallets then complain about these "stupid animals" that won't stay home. Folks, these animals have 24/7 to survey their situation, find weaknesses, and generally play havoc with your plans and sanity. They don't need to visit the doctor, go to school, get licenses or fill out mortgage paperwork. They are simply doing and being exactly what they were created and designed to do. Don't blame the pig.

To be charitable, I'm not saying all children are pigs, but the similarities are striking. Children don't have to talk to attorneys or pay taxes either. So they have lots of time to figure out the holes in our expectations. 'Nuff said. Direct them early and consistently and they'll usually give us less grief later on.

2. Each animal has a gift or talent that needs to be discovered and leveraged. They are quite different. For example, we use pigs to turn our compost. A big pig will dig down 3 feet deep. That's some serious pig power to oxygenate a compost pile.

A chicken likes to turn things too, but a hen doesn't have the strength of the pig. Her scratching is much more dainty. I wouldn't run pigs in an orchard even though they'd love to pick up dropped apples. They'd dig deep divots and expose fragile hair roots. Chickens are better because they're lighter and will still eat dropped fruit and bugs. But ducks. Now there's the orchardist's best friend.

Even among ducks, Indian Runners distinguish themselves for their voracious bug appetite and inability to scratch divots. You'd never ask a duck to turn compost, but ducks are perfect for gardens and orchards. But unless you have lots of ducks, they'll never keep up with the grass.

Cows eat the most grass, but they are heavy on the ground, often hurting tender tree root hairs in the top couple inches of soil. They also scratch, heavily, against trees. Too much damage. Sheep, the historically normal orchard and vineyard grazer, are much lighter on the ground and can't reach as high to nibble leaves or fruit.

I'll never forget being mesmerized for an hour in an olive grove north of San Francisco by a flock of goats pruning suckers. They literally climbed up 12 feet high in the trees, pruning all that inner sucker growth. They also mowed the grass under the trees. Certainly no other herbivore would climb 12 feet up into an olive tree and prune it for you. But a goat would never scrounge through a cow pie and eat out the fly maggots, either. Thank you, chickens, for that wonderful talent.

I could go on in this vein, but by now I think the point is clear: every animal has a unique, distinctive gift and it's up to us as their caretakers to place them in a habitat that will honor, respect, and leverage—affirm, perhaps?—the distinct gift. Wow. If that doesn't sound like something people could use toward each other, I don't know what does.

Every person has a gift, a unique ability. Starting with our children, we need to figure out what that gift is and feed its natural bent. People are different. Introverts and extroverts. Messies and cleanies. Savers and spenders. Starters and finishers. People who tend to be verbal and ones who like drawings.

I can't read a blueprint to save my soul. I'm completely verbal. But other people love blueprints; they want drawings. They don't want to hear me describe an Eggmobile; they want to see the blueprints. No animal is worthless. Each has something to contribute and if an animal is not contributing, usually it's because we failed, as caretakers, to honor its distinctiveness. Ditto for people.

Our culture is desperate for people-affirming vocations, noble visions, and sacred missions. We need writers and speakers, builders and dismantlers. We need engineers and prophets, scientists and poets. Imagine if as a society, in our marriages and families and our communities, we would put as much emphasis on honoring the specialness of people as much as we farmers honor the specialness of our animals. We'd never put a pig in the tomato patch. We'd never put a chicken in the dog pen. And yet we routinely squeeze people into boxes of performance and institutional trajectories because that's what society needs or expects, not because it's a context to facilitate flourishing. I could want to milk a pig forever, but I'll get a lot farther milking a cow.

3. Be gentle. Perhaps the most common admonition I need to give urban visitors to our farm, especially to children when they get around animals, is to not make sudden movements and to speak gently. Sudden anything scares animals. You don't have to be a Temple Grandin aficionado to understand this basic interactive axiom. Sudden anything frightens animals.

They respond to deliberate, systematic interaction. Perhaps the most advanced thing we do on our farm is sorting cows. Each cow has a flight zone and a cow can see about 330 degrees. You never want to come at a cow in her blind spot, right at her rear. As a prey animal, she thinks she's being attacked and will either take flight or whirl around where she can get a good look at you—and scare you to death in the process.

Cows move forward if you walk toward their shoulders. If you walk toward their neck, they'll back up. These responses are subtle enough that when you become a master of stockmanship, you can literally tilt your head and affect movement. Bud Williams, the late great guru of animal handling, always said if something isn't working, slow down. Frustrated? Slow down. Cattle won't go where you want them?

Slow down.

Sudden changes frighten people too. And yelling and screaming. You'll never get a cow settled if you're yelling and beating her. Ever. But if you scratch her tail head, rub behind her ears, coo gently, she'll quit quivering and gradually settle. Children respond the same way. And other people. In today's uncivil discourse, the ranting and raving in politics and racial divides, screaming and yelling, chanting and railing. Why? Be fun. Be gentle. Don't threaten and stomp. Coo. Where's the cooing politician? Jesus admonished that "the meek shall inherit the earth." He didn't say weak; He didn't say strong. He said meek, which is all about controlled strength.

We caretakers are certainly smarter than our animals. We can yell and strike and frighten. But we get along much better if we subjugate those base tendencies and move slowly, methodically, respectfully, quietly and gently. As our urban uninitiated visitors learn, it takes more strength to be gentle than to be bombastic and agitated. Perhaps the first rule of all presidential debates should be this: "talk like you're talking to your milk cow."

We can learn a lot from our animals, God bless 'em. I'm still learning every day because they have so much to teach me.

35

The Future

written in 2020

I may be turning into an old geezer, but I'm still loaded with dreams for the future. My partner bosses at *TMEN* wanted me to share some of my future projects and goals, so here you go.

1. Additional enterprises on our farm. What? You mean a dozen aren't enough? No, we haven't even scratched the surface. We'd like an autonomous produce/garden entrepreneur. We have land, compost, equipment, market, labor. What's not to love? Although Polyface is known for pastured livestock, we eat potatoes, blackberries, and zucchini too.

Success in any enterprise requires passion; few people are equally passionate about animals and plants. That dichotomy even extends to annuals versus perennials. Developing complementary enterprises with collaborative interests is the backbone of community, which is the path to resilience and security. Rounding out the grocery bag leverages our customers into bigger buyers and more dependency on us—the one stop farm.

I've picked out several perfect sites for orchards. We have

animals to keep it mowed and chippers to handle prunings. How about a vineyard? Specialty berries? Although we have most of this, it's not enough to feed our entire farm crew and we have plenty of customers who beg for more. I'm looking for a partner.

2. Food truck. This may actually happen this summer, but I've wanted to enter more value added food space for a long time. The farther down the food chain we can take our production, the less pressure on volume. Receiving income from more pieces of the food chain helps stabilize income. A mobile food venue that can travel to festivals, ball games and catering events takes the brand farther into the marketplace.

From a marketing standpoint, our farm team knows two sure ways to find customers: visiting the farm or eating the food. You either have to see it or taste it; once you do either of those, you're hooked. Some people can't imagine that I still have to think about marketing. Oh yes. Every day. All the time. The four horsemen of the apocalypse always threaten: divorce, death, disenfranchisement, and dislocation. The day you quit marketing is the day your business fails.

3. Clean food fast food. I've dreamed about this for 20 years, so it's not new. Wouldn't you love to be able to grab a grass-finished burger, locally sourced, chemical-free sweet potato fries and a kombucha drink anyplace where a McDonald's currently exists? This is a big dream, but if you don't write your dreams down and never talk about them, they'll never materialize. So I keep talking about this hoping that someday we'll be able to launch a prototype.

4. Fill up the land base. Our farm has infrastructure, expertise, and resources that could double production tomorrow if we had the market. We're working on the market, but the ship will come home when we actually leverage everything in our wheelhouse.

At some point, really authentic food needs to move past about 2 percent of the population. I'm not talking about faux organics, like hydroponics, factory chickens and desert mega-dairies. When Burger King announces a 10-year plan to start using cage-free eggs, why doesn't someone shout real loud: "You have a location 10 minutes from Polyface with eggs way better than cage free; why can't you make the change today?" But no, the press and stockholders go ga-ga over something as vapid and tepid as cage-free in 10 years.

The capacity for truly authentic food production is huge; I'm waiting for greenies to demand the real stuff and quit giving plaques to outfits like Burger King who can't buy a real egg right now. We need to fill up our potential.

5. Write more books. I've got a bunch of titles dancing around in my head. With two planned for release this year—both co-authored tomes—my next one (I think) will be something like *The Homestead Livestock Handbook*. You saw it first right here, folks. When I first began giving presentations more than 30 years ago, I'd finish and people would say "Oh, that's cute, but how does it scale up?" Today, when I get done, people say "Wow, that's awesome, but how does it scale down?"

Having been both tiny and today, a bigger outfit, I have no trouble moving seamlessly between large and small scale. But most folks can't make that shift. What does proper grazing management look like if I only have 2 cows on 3 acres and not

500 cows on 1,000 acres? What about health and hygiene? These days it seems like I spend a lot of time trying to apply Polyface to 5-10 acre places; this book will do that. I've always written to what folks ask about, their hot buttons. This book will be no different.

But other book titles include marketing and funny stories: "this really happened to me; it's funny today, but it wasn't funny then." Like you know it's going to be a bad day when 911 calls YOU. I got four chapters into a novel a couple of years ago and gave up; fiction is tough. With non-fiction, I don't have to invent anything. With fiction, I've got to invent everything, and that's hard. So we'll see.

6. Composting toilet. We have 15,000 visitors a year to our farm. In 2020, with the *TMEN* fair coming, that might spike this year. Hope you're planning to come. See, always marketing. But I digress. We've used porta-potties for years but I don't like those things. Regulations regarding composting toilets all but prohibit installing them in our area.

Our farmstead is on low ground so installing a water-based septic system is problematic; we'd have to pump everything uphill. I love composting toilets and have seen some great designs in Australia that would work. They're not legal, but I've never worried too much about that. I want a true gnome structure: living roof with cascading cucumber vines growing all around it. So you go into a jungle to do your business. And it's all hidden from bureaucrats.

7. McDonald's and Chick-fil-A start closing stores. This is the only negative goal on here, but I'm waiting for the day when these bastions of everything that's wrong in our food supply finally begin closing their doors. I'm going to be a happy camper that day. Right now I don't care if it happens because people begin eating at home or begin eating at my clean food, fast food alternative. All I know is that as long as these outfits keep expanding, we're continuing to go the wrong way.

8. Polyface Hot Pockets. Integrity convenience is the only really accelerating segment of the food system. Thirty years ago I predicted that by now everybody would rediscover their kitchens. I was 100 percent wrong. Goodness, the meal kit fad has already tanked because people say they don't have time to cook the kit.

But do you know how hard it is to get a legal Hot Pocket? Government regulations are a nightmare. They certainly don't give us food safety; what they give us is market access to special large and well-connected processors. One day, though, one day we're going to have Polyface Hot Pockets.

9. A new amendment to the Bill of Rights guaranteeing every American citizen the right to acquire the food of their choice from the source of their choice. In a time when we kick the government out of our bedrooms, our weddings, and our pregnancies, I'm waiting for the day when we kick the government out of our stomachs.

When will consenting adults practicing voluntary freedom of choice be able to purchase raw milk, homemade charcuterie, and backyard summer sausage? The apparent abundance in today's supermarkets is a pittance of what could and should be available if cottage industry entrepreneurs were unleashed on their neighborhoods in true food sovereignty.

Recently I spoke in a California university and asked the

students: "How many of you think a government official should inspect and license your ability to eat a carrot from your own garden in order to insure food safety?" A quarter of the hands in that lecture hall went up. I was stunned. It almost incited a riot as the detractors looked incredulously at these folks wanting that level of governmental oversight. Where has freedom gone?

I'm looking for the day when we care as much about food freedom as we do about gun freedom. When we care as much about freedom to participate in neighborhood food commerce as we do about participating in the bathrooms of our choice.

10. Build more ponds. Hydration is the foundation of functional ecology. Water is the beginning of life. Most of the planet is aridifying; you can almost feel the earth's mouth parched, dry, and begging for water. North America 500 years ago was 8 percent water thanks to 400 million beavers. It's time to restore that abundance-generating landscape.

I have pond sites picked out all over our farm. Every time we get a couple thousand extra dollars, I call in our favorite excavator and build another pond. Functionally, these ponds reduce flooding and offer irrigation in dry times. Beyond that, they offer spectacular riparian habitat for wildlife and aquatic plants and animals. They stimulate cloud formation and ambient temperature stability. And they're beautiful.

Ultimately, we can never finish making our landscape more beautiful, more resilient, more productive. Nature always has more to give than we can imagine. Those are some of my dreams; what are yours?

36

Reducing Energy

written in 2020

Half of the expenses on the average farm in America is energy and most of that is for fuel. Several years ago as fuel prices spiked and I read those statistics in farm publications, I decided to see how our farm compared. Ours was only 5 percent, and that included two delivery trucks we run about 4 days a week. At the time, we determined that diesel fuel could go to $10 a gallon and we'd still be fine. Although we still use plenty of fuel, we're consoled knowing we'll be the last guy standing when everything falls apart.

While this difference in percentage doesn't necessarily translate to profitability, it certainly does reflect a degree of resiliency. Reducing energy consumption and dependency offers numerous benefits. But how do we do it? Here are some strategic protocols.

1. Reduce feedstock transportation. Bulky feeds like hay should never be transported to the animals; instead, transport the animals to the hay. Ideally we feed hay proximate to where we made it.

Many years ago we outgrew our single barn and decided to build a second one. Orthodox thinking would put the new one near the old one, clustering the farm's infrastructure to utilize existing roads, water lines, and power. But on our farm, all that farmstead cluster is not centrally located. As a result, we built the new barn toward the far end of the property.

That way when we make hay, we have two options for storage, greatly reducing transport energy. In the spring, when we spread the compost generated by that hay feeding, we have close fields to receive it. That further reduces run time.

Decentralized infrastructure, strategically located to reduce haul time, saves not only energy but time as well. Multiple structures, duplicated, offer more storage and feed out options.

2. Coordinate trips across the field. Trips with machinery are expensive. "Go loaded and come loaded" is a phrase we use all the time to plan our vehicle movements for greatest advantage. This is why our pastured poultry enterprises have on-board or proximate mobile feed storage.

By inventorying feed on site, we can carefully plan re-fills to times when we need to go out anyway. Or we can fill several feed boxes at a time. One start, make a loop around the various containers, and return home. In the course of a year, saving 30 or 40 single-function trips and machinery startups adds up to huge energy savings.

One of the biggest energy uses is the notorious trip to town. How many errands can we run in the same trip? With conscious planning, can we drop trips to town from two a week to one a week? This alone can save thousands of dollars a year in fuel costs.

3. Substitute human labor for machinery. On our farm, the most obvious example of this is our lightweight highly mobile pastured chicken shelters. The most common complaint about this model is labor to move the shelters. As a result, folks try to use garden tractors, front end loaders, or design bigger ones that require a tractor—anything to get away from human labor to pull the shelters along.

We have yet—and we've tried—to find a single alternative using machinery that beats our human labor in time spent per chicken. When you add in the cost of machinery, the trip to the field, the upkeep of the road, the deterioration of multiple tracks across the field, substituting human labor for equipment can often pay big energy-savings dividends.

Numerous gardening techniques are beginning to make the conventional tiller obsolete. From J.M. Fortier's tarps to Paul Gautschi's deep wood chips to ergonomically designed broadforks, many gardeners scarcely use gas-powered machinery any more. Who needs a Peleton when you can ride a broadfork for an hour? I love my broadfork; it's a great workout and leaves the most beautiful soil bed in the world. If the soil is in good condition, you can cover a lot of ground in short order.

A couple of years ago we tried experimenting with bringing firewood in long lengths to the wood pile and cutting it there. Picking up the long lengths with the front end loader forks, loading them on a wood cart, then unloading them, and then stumbling and tripping over the pile while cutting them up with the chainsaw—it's actually more efficient to whack up the pieces in the woods and load them onto a trailer by hand. A dump trailer makes it even more efficient. Many times a little sweat beats a machine; not always, for sure, but sometimes. Look for those sweet spots where hands can compete.

4. Pastured livestock. Keeping animals outside reduces costs of hauling manure and ventilating structures. Concentrated Animal Feeding Operations use enormous amounts of energy running massive fans, hauling manure, and heating in the winter time. Pasturing eliminates all those elements and provides additional benefits like sanitation, fresh air, exercise, and saliva to stimulate pruned grass growth.

Certainly anyone with livestock will want to house them protectively from time to time. On our farm, chickens, rabbits, and pigs enjoy winter housing in hoop houses, each situated lengthwise west to east to capture westerly breezes. Rather than one or two huge structures, we have 5 smaller ones (30 ft. X 120 ft.) that are sized to operate with natural ventilation. If they were bigger, we couldn't get enough airflow through them with natural flow.

Extending the grazing season through management intensity (moving animals every day or two) is the single biggest energy and cost saver with herbivores. In our area, the average farmer feeds hay for 120 days per year. Our average is 40 days per year. That is all hay you don't have to mow, rake, bale, store, and haul. Observant readers will notice a pattern developing here: what saves energy also generally saves time. The two go hand in hand.

5. Never haul water. Pipe is cheap. Pumps are cheap. Water is heavy. Many farmers spend accumulated days per year waiting for tanks to fill, ferrying water out to fields. I know. I used to do it too. Then I discovered black plastic pipe. Wow, what a game changer.

Our farm now has 8 miles of 1 1/4 inch pipe cris-crossing and surrounding every field. Every 100 yards a valve offers clean, pressurized water. With today's technology, nobody can justify the energy required to move water in a tank.

One of the principles of permaculture is to locate buildings on high ground in order to capture roof run-off and then gravity flow it to lower elevations. I don't like wells because they poke holes in the aquifer and they start with water that must be pumped from inventory located far below the ground. On our farm, we've built ponds in valleys up on high ground and our 8 mile system enjoys gravity flow; no pumps, no electricity, no switches. As long as gravity works, the water runs. When gravity quits, I'm out of here.

How long does black plastic pipe last? Perhaps 200 years? Although plastic is made out of petroleum, the one-time energy cost is nothing compared to toting water day after day after day. Trust me, you'll never regret installing pipe and parking the water buggy.

6. Let animals do the work. What can animals do that you would normally use equipment to do? On our farm, the best illustration is turning compost with pigs. When we feed hay, we bed the cows with wood chips and junk hay, creating a fermenting anaerobic pile. As we add bedding, we also add whole shelled corn. When the cows return to pasture in the spring, we turn in pigs. They seek the imbedded fermented corn, flinging the material as they dig. This aeration converts the pile to a beautiful oxygenated compost without any machinery whatsoever.

Eliminating brush with goats rather than machinery is another example of using animals to do our work. Debugging with chickens, guinea fowl, or ducks enables work to occur in a location without us having to be there. That means we don't have to drive there.

7. Heat with wood. My house is heated with an outdoor wood-fired water stove. In fact, it heats Mom's house too. That one unit saves us $10,000 in electricity and fuel oil each year. Some of the best income we earn each year is displacing purchased energy with our own home-grown solar collectors: trees. I agree with the homesteader who said that if gasoline supplies dwindle to one gallon on the planet, it should go through a chain saw. I get the shakes every time I realize that the chainsaw as we know it is only as old as I am. Wow, what a great time to be alive.

For the record, I'm certainly in favor of solar panels, windmills, biogas, hydro turbines, tides and any other kind of alternative energy conceivable. But we all know the biggest and quickest way to reduce petroleum-based energy is to simply use less energy, period. The more all of us can do that, the more wiggle room we have to develop the alternatives. And the farther those alternatives will go.

I'm still hoping for hydrogen. I want a windmill-powered hydrogen electrolysis machine on my farm pond sending hydrogen over to a tank on the shore. Then I convert all my trucks and tractors to run on hydrogen. That's my dream. What's yours?

37

Farm Entertainment

written in 2020

Too often people think a farm is boring, a place of drudgery that can't possibly feed the creative and adventuresome human spirit. When the editors at *TMEN* asked me to write about creativity, music, and art on the farm, I first felt inadequate to the task since I'm known as a workaholic. Who wants to publicize diversions from the farm? I'm trying to get people to love the farm for the farm's sake; since I love my work, I don't need to escape from it.

Bud Williams, famous cow whisperer, always said that if you have to get away to be fulfilled, don't come back. But the little ditty "all work and no play makes Johnny a dull boy" is also true, especially for children. So what kind of diversions offer outlets for entertainment and artistic expressions here on our farm? When I started making a list, I found a lot of things that fit this category. And I found out maybe I'm not a workaholic after all.

Let's start with the children. Since we had no TV and homeschooled, you might think our kids grew up deprived. We didn't do little league sports, ballet, or other more normal urban creativity exercises. But my childhood, our kids', and now our grandchildren's lives are full of forts, tree houses, and creek dams.

What could possibly compete with using some old pallets, baler twine and scrap lumber to build a play area? Whenever urban friends visited, guess where they went, happily, for hours? Out to the forts. With a proper cloth flag waving triumphantly overtop, a home-made fort represents the pinnacle of young imagination. We have a massive woodpile by the outdoor wood furnace; a bit of shoving and repositioning by children turns it into a defensive fortress. Duct tape a flag on a broom handle and it's official.

And what about a hay mow with small square bales? The mother of all playgrounds, a hay mow with tunnels through the bales and ropes hanging from the rafters beats anything a gym could ever provide. Great exercise. Oh, the friendships forged and make-believe enemies vanquished in these imaginative play areas are the stuff of memories, imagination, and wisdom (learning the difference between death and just adrenaline rush).

Tree houses are another simple but functional entertain-ment area. Never put a bolt or nail in a tree; all of ours use undergirding lashed with nylon rope. But getting up off the ground gives a youngster a perspective they don't get often—being the highest rather than the lowest. My favorite play place growing up was in a massive pear tree that had a perfect crotch above a tree house that seemed like just the right cockpit for an airplane. Who needs video games when you can fly a peach tree over Tokyo?

Today on our farm we have an honest-to-goodness playground for customers and visitors who come. A teeter-totter, tire swing, living tee-pee (pole beans on simple pyramidal trellis) and the best, a corn box. You can play in a sand box anywhere, but on a farm, we have a corn box. It's about 12 ft. X 12 ft., covered, and contains about 18 inches of whole shelled yellow corn (nonGMO). With some children's excavation toys in there, it's magnetic for kids. Parents collect their children after literally hours of play; the kids come out covered in corn dust but faces lit up smiling (or crying because they don't want to leave).

This play area is in a shady spot under some trees and includes several picnic tables. Few respites are as enjoyable as a picnic. Over the years, we've developed picnic spots on the farm and they all hold special memories. The first one was up by a creek where my aunt and I stepped on a rattlesnake when she was visiting from Indiana. When we finally installed the road up the mountain (2 miles long) we created two picnic areas, complete with outhouses, where we could go as family or with friends and get away.

Now that our farm family includes apprentices, stewards and additional permanent staff, these picnic areas create places for story telling, whittling, and of course music. Someone brings a guitar and regales us with live entertainment. We've had numerous musically talented visitors to the farm as well and we generally offer them a meal in exchange for an impromptu concert.

One of the most unusual was a three-man band called Moon Hooch; a percussionist and two saxophonists. They called me one day and asked if they could play for our cows. Their performance has gotten more than 600,000 views on YouTube under Moon Hooch Cattle Dance Party July 11, 2013. You can't make this stuff up. Who says you can't have fun on a farm?

One of the most creative things I did for the children when

they were small was a birthday treasure hunt. I hid clues all over the farm. Each clue sent them to another spot where they had to find the clue. Eventually they found the treasure, but it took a couple of hours going all over the farm to get to the end. Of course, they had to know where north, south, east, and west were in order to understand the next leg in the process.

Without TV (still don't have one) we spent a lot, and I mean a LOT, of time reading aloud. I've repeated that now with my grandchildren. What makes reading aloud come alive? Losing yourself. Making faces and different voice tones make stories live for children. It's true blue theater, but the secret is to lose yourself. Some of the first exercises in drama school revolve around getting over being self-conscious about how you look to others.

Reading with emphasis and dramatic flair is more entertaining, and takes more creativity, than anyone can imagine. It still does, regardless of what's on the electronic screen. Some of the best off-farm entertainment is the community theater. You can either join as an actor or support cast, or you can just attend the performances. In either case, exposing kids to literature and drama feeds the imagination. Literature and stories are the stuff of world awareness, whether you physically travel it or not.

Of course, in our family, much of our away-from-the-farm time revolves around farming conferences and visiting other farmers. Along the way, we enjoy museums and nature attractions. When you have livestock, the hardest part of getting away is not the going; it's the caretaking at home. Our stories of farm-sitters could fill a book.

The kinds of things that can happen while you're gone prove that truth is stranger than fiction. Wheels fall off. Stuff burns down. One time when we flew to Texas for a time away we had scarcely started the first flight when a wind storm came and blew one of the covers off one of our hoop houses. The two apprentices suddenly had more to handle than they ever bargained for, but we talked them through options on the phone and they gradually got things triaged enough to not lose the farm.

Back when I was a kid and we didn't have apprentices, our farm-sitters were city friends. Boy howdy. From the cow kicking over the milk bucket to spilling all the eggs stepping out of the chicken house, these friends could have made Funniest Home Videos at our expense. Training up a neighbor or friend to be familiar with your operation is probably a bigger issue than deciding where to go or what to do. Investing in a farm sitter to enable a trip may be the best investment you make in the whole year.

Finally, farms today enjoy a mystique revival. Seeking connections to the land and nostalgic experiences, many people yearn to come to a farm for events. Whether it's a simple concert, meal, dramatic presentation or Easter Egg Hunt, you as a farmer can enjoy a cosmopolitan nexus at home. That's pretty cool. Hosting an event puts you in touch with community leaders and artists you would never meet otherwise. Our farm hosted a Plein Air event for a couple of years and fed them. That's a sophisticated bunch.

Tap into your local experts. We have a neighbor who is one of the foremost ornithologists in the U.S. We invite him over for supper and he entertains us with bird songs and information. We call it singing for supper. A community has all sorts of expertise and storytellers. A local historian, poet, business owner—almost any topic and any person can be interesting with a dab of passion and verve.

Think back about how folks entertained themselves in the *Little House on the Prairie* series. Towns had spelling bees, mock political debates, and dramatic recitations. They made their own fun, if not corporately, then in the home as a family. A farm is the best place for this kind of entertainment because you don't disturb the neighbors. What better place for revelry than a farm?

38

Legacy Anchors

written in 2020

These are disturbing times. History will tell whether they are more disturbing than other times. Think about living during the American Revolution. Or the Civil War. Or Oct. 9, 1929. Or Pearl Harbor. DDT. "I Have a Dream." Viet Nam. Woodstock. The Food Pyramid. 9/11. TSA. Desert Storm. Impeachment. And now coronavirus, burning cities, and a rancorous presidential election.

On a scale of disturbance, 2020 will go down in history as a big one. These disturbances are unsettling. Although we never know what the future holds, when things are rocking along on an even keel, we don't think about it much. I've always said that as long as the NFL is on TV, beer is in the fridge, and the paycheck is steady most folks are pretty chill.

But in 2020, all three of those things have faltered and people are concerned at least and hysterically paranoid at worst. As I write this I feel like I'm in a time bubble where January was a century ago and December is still a century away. In times of unease, I appreciate legacy anchors in my life.

1. Relationships. Family and friends offer steadiness in times that seem unmoored. On our farm, we have four generations living and loving together; that's extremely rare in these transient and tumultuous times.

During Y2K many people embraced a prepper mentality; that tribe is still alive and well. Perhaps 2020 is Y2K on steroids. With empty supermarket shelves, mandatory mask wearing and a daily ticker counting deaths, people are rediscovering the value of close relationships.

The fact that I can walk our entire farm and remember being on every square foot with dad is a wonderful memory and steadying hand. That we are now doing projects we only dreamed about 30 years ago creates continuity in a time of disruption.

2. Tools. Few elements define a homestead more than the tools in the shop. Old and well-worn tools speak of longevity, care, and shared tasks. My nostalgic favorite in our shop are my dad's oil stones with his name embossed on the wooden casings. He taught me how to sharpen knives and by my teenage years I no longer needed his assistance.

My eyes still tear up remembering that rite of passage nearly 50 years ago when he handed me those stones, passing ownership from his hands to mine. A ton of gold could not be more valuable because this bequest affirmed mastery and dependability. I still oil my chainsaw file with the oil can I squirted on the metal drill as he pushed it through a piece of steel. As a 5-year-old standing on a 5-gallon bucket to reach the vice that held the steel, my little oil squirts affirmed my importance. When I pick up that little oil can, it represents a couple of lifetimes. And now my grandchildren use it. That little oil can spans four generations; it's an icon of steadiness in a topsy turvy world.

A family homestead offers these kinds of anchors, and the longer the homestead thrives, the more profound the steadiness. There's the shovel we used to plant the grape vines. That's the pitchfork—yes, the one with the worn down tines—that we used to clean out the hay bunk. There sit the wedges we used to split posts before we bought the band sawmill. These tools provide a mental and emotional haven during cultural storms.

3. Infrastructure. Few homestead components offer more comfort than buildings. The equipment shed and tool shed have their place, but the best one is the barn. Few things conjure up more memories, both painful and ecstatic, than barns. That's where the calf we doctored finally died. Tears and consoling in the arms of a parent vividly imprint their emotional trauma on our memories.

But barns are also the place of miracles. That breach calf that slid out and shook its head, signifying "I'll be just fine, thank you very much." Or that weak calf we held on our knee and squirted milk into its mouth. When the calf suddenly convulsed in recognition, latched onto the teat, and drew long, life-giving suckles; oh, the wonder, the mystery, the strength of life.

When all about society fixates on death and doom, a walk into that barn with its sweet smells and life abundance breathes contentment into our soul. The barn holds deep conversations. "Why did the lamb die?" "How does the cat move her kittens?" "Why do the cows like this hay but not that hay?" These are life foundation questions and spawn the lingo legacy we tell our kids. "Dad used to say" or "Mom always said . . . ."

Those memories come from the kitchen, the barn, the field where working together we learn to live in servanthood. The hallowed buildings, under these roofs, the hush of night and rush of morning, the stillness of sleep and the cacophony of morning rooster crows: all of this offers us the gift of continuity. The assurance that life goes on.

4. Landscape. People make home in every kind of climate and culture you can imagine. I'm often asked about what constitutes the perfect homestead. Urban refugees worry about finding the right place. My standard answer is that ultimately we make the place perfect. You can be in a desert or a swamp, but if your creativity is operating and your passion is at peak, you will figure out how to turn anyplace into a wonderful place.

On our farm, the first names given to fields stick for generations. Our "field by Jim" pays homage to our neighbor who lived and died next door. Though he passed away many years ago, we still call it the "field by Jim." He hasn't been around for a long time, but his spirit lives on in the fields, fences, and buildings he maintained.

We have a massive oak tree that was in a field edge long before our family arrived in 1961. After we arrived, we let the forest grow up around it and today we've recovered that old overgrown field and turned it back into a nice pasture. It's called "the squirrel tree field." We called that white oak the squirrel tree because when we were kids and started our forays into hunting traditions, we could always find a couple of squirrels running up and down that tree.

Although it is in decline and a good forester would no doubt cut it down before the lumber goes bad, I can't for the life of me bring myself to cut it down. It's majestic, imposing its crown high into the heavens. And yes, it still has squirrels even though I don't go out with my little .410. That gun went to my son when he started hunting, and now he has given it to my grandson. Such is the legacy of landscapes; they define our activities.

Over time landscapes change. Our caress on this ecological womb defines how those changes occur. For many years we had a thin-soiled ridge that had a little square that seemed as fertile as the creek-side meadow. That's the spot where the old manure spreader broke down and I had to shovel it out by hand. That extra heavy load of compost changed that spot forever.

When our minds become preoccupied with societal disturbance and worry, a walk amidst our handiwork is a balm for the soul. A change here, a new activity there, and suddenly the landscape responds with a tree, a mushroom, a luxuriant patch of red clover. The landscape carries on.

5. Genetics. Perhaps nothing speaks of nostalgic legacy as powerfully as plant and animal genetics. These not only bridge human generations; they bridge other generations.

On our farm, our favorite one is a tomato that my wife Teresa's grandmother saved from her mother. Grandma saved the seeds from year to year and as she aged and quit keeping a big garden, she always planted several of those tomatoes right by her back door. She'd put a trellis up alongside the farmhouse and they'd climb up eight feet. I remember one year she kept weighing the tomatoes off of one plant and the cumulative total came to more than 100 pounds.

When we got married, Teresa got some of those seeds from her grandmother and has planted them faithfully every year now for forty years in our own garden and they are just as healthy, productive, and tasty as we remember them in Grandma's kitchen. So burn the cities. Shut down the businesses. Fill the hospitals. We have an unnamed family heirloom tomato that survived two world wars, Viet Nam, and the coronavirus. In 2020, it's bearing profusely, seemingly oblivious to the uncertainty and disruption occurring all around us.

The cow that looks like her great-great-grandmother of two decades ago doesn't care a lick about face masks and unemployment figures. She just does her thing, pruning the forage, chewing her cud, licking my extended hand with her sandpaper tongue. That's contentment. Stewarding life in all its forms provides comfort and serenity in an otherwise chaotic world.

Those of us who farm and homestead can offer many reasons to do it. They include the hyper-practical like food security, but they also include the emotional-spiritual soothing that comes from indomitable life. This is life that we can touch, smell, see, and taste, offering legacy anchors when storms toss society's ship into uncertain waters. For that reason alone, I recommend homesteading.

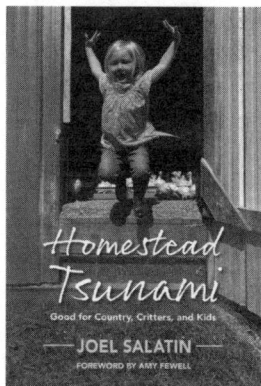

Homestead Tsunami: Good for Country, Critters and Kids (2023)

In good times or bad, having some control of our basic needs reduces worry and fear. Social, cultural, and physical disturbances are making more people ready to protect our families, fortunes, and faith through homesteading. From food security to healthy, happy kids, functional homesteads heal on multiple fronts. The rewards are worth the effort. Find out why.

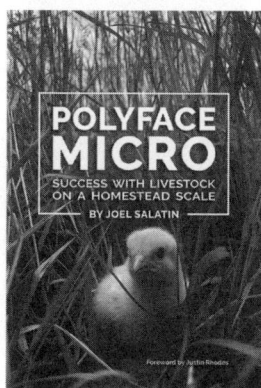

Polyface Micro: Success with Livestock on a Homestead Scale (2021)

Success with domestic livestock does not require large land bases. Polyface Farm leads the world in animal-friendly and ecologically authentic, commercial, pasture-based livestock production. In *Polyface Micro* Joel adapts the ideas and protocols to small holdings. Homesteaders can increase production, enjoy healthy animals, and create aesthetically and aromatically pleasant livestock systems.

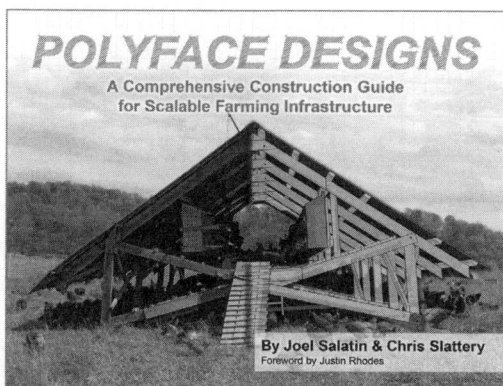

Polyface Designs: A Comprehensive Construction Guide for Scalable Farming Infrastructure (2020)

A comprehensive how-to manual of Polyface Farm's signature designs-with tips, tricks, and a half century of lessons learned through trial and error. Joel wrote the text and Polyface former apprentice and engineer extraordinaire Chris Slattery created the diagrams. Full color and beautiful enough to be a coffee table book even though you'll use it in your shop.

Other Books by Joel Salatin

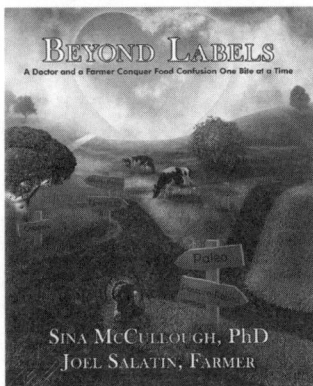

Beyond Labels: A Doctor and a Farmer Conquer Food Confusion One Bite at a Time (2020)

Joel Salatin and Sina McCullough bring you on a journey from generally unhealthy food and farming to an ultimately healing place. This book is designed to meet you where you are and motivate you to take the next step in your healing journey – ultimately bringing you closer to health, happiness, and freedom.

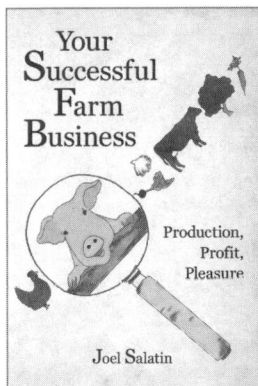

Your Successful Farm Business: Production, Profit, Pleasure (2017)

The sequel to Joel's *You Can Farm* builds on another 20 years of experience as Polyface Farm progressed from a small family operation to a 20-person, 6,000-customer, 50-restaurant business, all without sales targets, government grants, or an off-farm nest egg. Salatin offers a pathway to success, with production, profit, and pleasure thrown in for good measure.

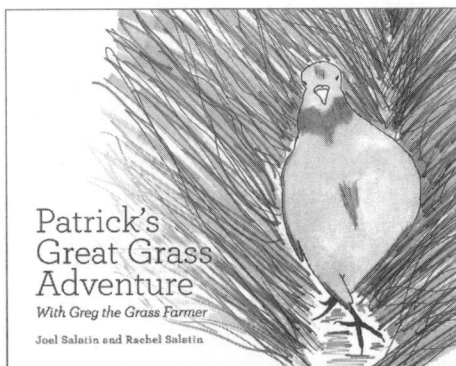

Patrick's Great Grass Adventure: With Greg the Grass Farmer (2017)

In his first children's book, Joel and his daughter Rachel Salatin team up on a whimsical tale about a pigeon, a farmer, and grass. Beautifully illustrated it introduces 4-7 year-olds to Greg the grass farmer through the eyes of Patrick Pigeon. What better way to discover ecology-enhancing grass farming than from an aerial view? Discover a real farm from a real farmer through captivating explanation and illustration.

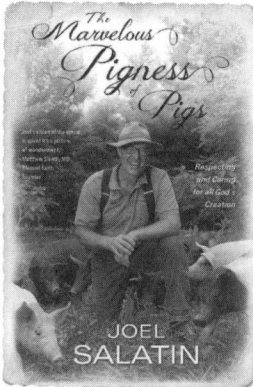

The Marvelous Pigness of Pigs: Nurturing and Caring for All God's Creation (2016)

Growing up straddling the tension between the environmental and faith-based community, Joel pokes good-naturedly at the stereotypes with his self-acclaimed moniker: Christian libertarian environmentalist capitalist lunatic farmer. The question is simple: Do the beliefs in the pew align with what's on the menu?

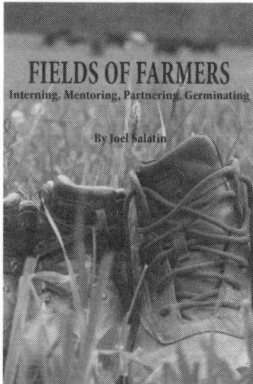

Fields of Farmers: Interning, Mentoring, Partnering, Germinating (2013)

America's average farmer is 60 years old. Our culture needs a generational transfer of millions of farm acres facing abandonment, development, or amalgamation into ever-larger holdings. Based on experience with interns and multigenerational partnerships, Joel digs into the problems and solutions surrounding this land and knowledge-transfer crisis. This book empowers aspiring farmers, and nonfarming landlords to build regenerative, profitable agricultural enterprises.

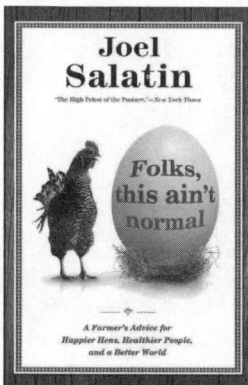

Folks, This Ain't Normal: A Farmer's Advice for Happier Hens, Healthier People, and a Better World (2012)

Joel discusses how far removed we are from the simple, sustainable joy that comes from living close to the land and the people we love. Salatin understands what food should be: Wholesome, seasonal, raised naturally, procured locally, prepared lovingly, and eaten with a profound reverence for the circle of life.

Other Books by Joel Salatin

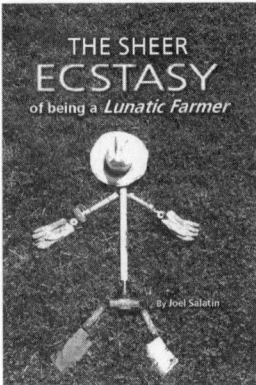

The Sheer Ecstasy of Being a Lunatic Farmer (2010)

Can there really be that much difference between the way two farmers operate? After all, a cow is a cow and the land is the land, isn't it? Gleaning stories from his fifty years as localized, compost-fertilized, pasture-based, beyond organic farmer, Joel explores the differences. From how farmers view soil and water, to how they build fences, market their products or involve their families, Salatin explains a different food model and shows with good humor and stories how this alleged lunacy actually offers a life of sheer ecstasy.

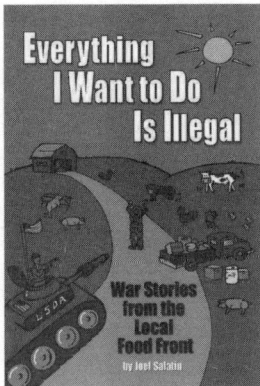

Everything I Want to Do Is Illegal: War Stories from the Local Food Front (2007)

Although Polyface Farm has been glowingly featured in national print and video media, it would not exist if the USDA and the Virginia Department of Agriculture and Consumer Services had their way. From a lifetime of noncompliance, frustration, humor, and passion come the behind-the-scenes real stories that brought this family farm into the forefront of the non-industrial food system.

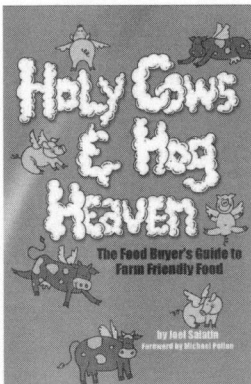

Holy Cows and Hog Heaven: The Food Buyer's Guide to Farm Friendly Food (2004)

Written to empower food buyers in their dedication to food with integrity. Farmers who give it to their customers say that folks who have read it have a new level of understanding and a delightful attitude about the farmer-consumer relationship. Insights and real-life stories shared from Joel's own marketing experience.

Other Books by Joel Salatin

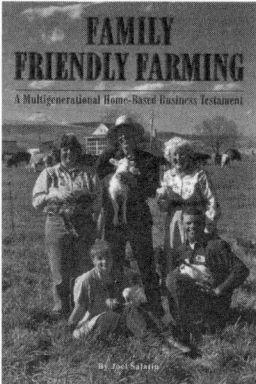

Family Friendly Farming: A Multi-Generational Home-Based Business Testament (2001)

Few life circumstances are as hard to navigate as family business. This book describes the rules and relational principles to harmonize in what is too often a tense environment. The chapters on how to get your children to enjoy working with you are worth the price of the book. Beyond that, it delves into the quagmire of inheritance, family meetings, and personal responsibility. A pathway exists to leverage the strengths of family business and hold families, and especially family farms, together.

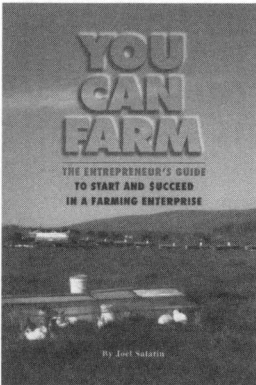

You Can Farm: The Entrepreneur's Guide to Start and $ucceed in a Farming Enterprise (1997)

Joel pulls from his eclectic sphere of knowledge, combines it with a half century of farming experience, and covers as many topics as he can think of that will affect the success of a farming venture. He offers his 10 best picks for profitable ventures, and the 10 worst. If this book scares you off, it will be the best reality check you ever bought.

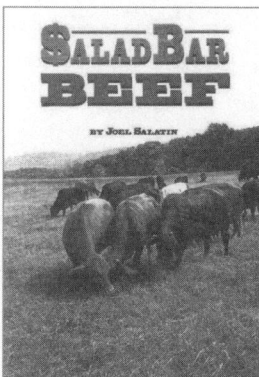

$alad Bar Beef (1995)

Fishing for a phrase to describe this ultimately land-healing and nutrition-escalating production model, Joel coined the phrase Salad Bar to describe the farm's beef. Learn about herd effect, mobbing, moving, field design, water systems, manure monitoring, soil fertility, and even pigaerating. A fundamentally fresh way to look at the symbiosis between farmer, field, and cow. A classic in the pasture-based livestock movement.

Other Resources by Joel Salatin

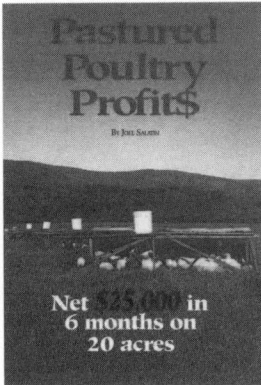

Pastured Poultry Profit$: Net $25,000 on 20 Acres in 6 Months (1993)

Joel began raising chickens when he was 10 years old and fell into the pastured poultry concept a couple of years later. Still the engine that drives sales, notoriety, and profit, pastured poultry has revolutionized countless farming endeavors around the world. A how-to book, it includes all the stories and tips, from brooding to marketing. Centered around meat chickens, it includes a section on layers and turkeys. This book started the American pastured poultry movement.

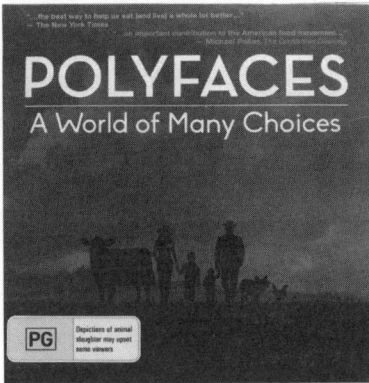

Polyfaces: A World of Many Choices DVD (2015)

One Australian family spent 4 years documenting a style of farming that will help change the fate of humanity! It follows the Salatin's, a 4th generation farming family as they produce food in a way that works with nature, not against it. Set amidst the stunning Shenandoah Valley in Virginia, 'Polyface Farm' is led by "the world's most innovative farmer" (TIME) and uses no chemicals and feeds over 6,000 families and many restaurants and food outlets within a 3 hour 'food-shed' of their farm. This model is being replicated, proving that we can provide quality produce without depleting our planet. (1 hour 32 minutes).

242

Other Resources by Joel Salatin

The Salatin Semester: A Complete Homestudy Course in Polyface-Style Diversified Farming

This multimedia production conveys the Salatin family's methods of profitable diversified farming like no other. Joel Salatin presents his farming system in professional edited, live-cut video, engaging audio, and in a detail-rich reference guide. Live presentations are presented in DVD video; audio interviews with Q&A are in digital audio; and the myriad questions and answers from the resulting discussion are transcribed and edited in a detailed reference guide. The end result is an amazingly extensive – and affordable – training guide to help you reinvent your farm. :

- 18 hours of video on 12 DVDs
- 6 hours of audio Q&A
- Digital slideshow farm tour
- 256-page guidebook

Primer Series: Pigs 'n Glens DVD (2013)

Pigs are omnivores, like humans. This video combines the most ancient hog production techniques with the best of modern technology, using pigs to massage the ecological landscape in exercise.
Released June 2013 (40 minutes).

Primer Series: Techno Stealth: Metropolitan Buying Clubs DVD (2014)

Over the years, we developed a local food distribution system that we call the Metropolitan Buying Club. It combines the real-time interfaces of online marketing with community-based interaction. These kinds of interfaces create efficiencies and economies of scale in local food distribution.
Released July 2014 (45 minutes).

The Polyface Farm DVD (1998)

This is the official, comprehensive video about the farm. Carefully filmed and edited by Moonstar Films over the course of a year to catch the multi-faceted seasons and enterprises at Polyface, this was a monumental effort and a delightful artistic piece. You will see Joel and Daniel in each section, talking and working in everyday settings. Released 1998 (110 minutes).

Other Resources by Joel Salatin

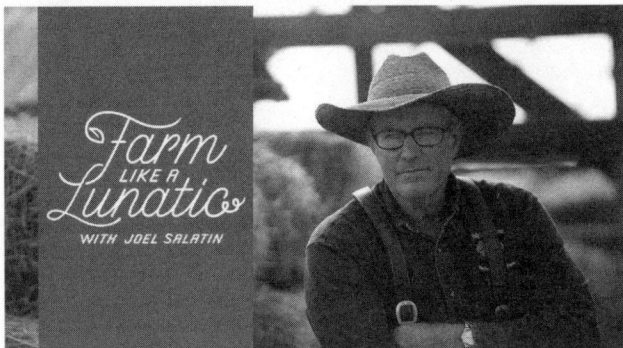

Farm Like A Lunatic

An ongoing video curriculum, this video series is a joint effort between Polyface Farm and lilDRAGON.tv, a production company out of Tennessee. Currently offering 25 hours of content, the goal is to eventually hit 100 hours. Joel personally writes and oversees the instructional material. Courses currently include:

- Pastured Broilers
- Carbonaceous Diaper
- Salad Bar Beef
- Pastured Pigs
- Pastured Laying Hens
- Cattle Grazing Management
- Farm Direct Marketing

The goal is to expand the course over the next few years to include many more aspects of Polyface Farm and Joel's lifetime experience. While this curriculum is geared toward making a living as a commercial farmer, many farm enterprises start as homesteads and then expand. This course thematically honors that potential in progress, serving both large and small scale pursuits.

www.farmlikealunatic.com

Joel Salatin's Books & Videos Available From

Polyface Farm Gift Shop	1-540-885-3590	www.polyfacefarms.com
Chelsea Green Publishing		www.chelseagreen.com
Amazon		www.amazon.com
Your local bookstore		

244